Praise for *Slice Harvester*

"*Slice Harvester* stands out from the pack . . . wry, witty, surprisingly insightful . . . [Hagendorf's] ability to veer from the profane to the profound in the same sentence is as unique as it is grounded in the punk-lit tradition. Among all the things that *Slice Harvester* seeks and succeeds to be, it's a love letter to Manhattan—one stained with spilled beer and cigarette burns, but still. It's also about chasing ideals, romantic as well as culinary, and how that can be both noble and annihilating. Mostly, though, it's a rumination on innocence, and the loss thereof. Deep stuff for a book that started out as a pizza blog. Then again, as *Slice Harvester* so compellingly proposes, the plain old pizza pie is actually a blank canvas upon which we can, and should, project anything we wish."

—*NPR Books*

"His blog, Slice Harvester, documents his efforts to eat a plain slice from every pizzeria in Manhattan. The amazing thing isn't that he claims to have accomplished this goal—though it took him twenty-seven months—but that the blog, with its star system and unlikely metaphors, made for such good reading. It makes an even better book. His sauce-stained slog is no longer just about finding good slices but also (though the antiestablishment Hagendorf would surely hate the phrase) about finding himself . . . The pizza joints become potent way stations along the journey and, thanks to a neat surprise involving the origins of one shop, acquire a strong narrative arc."

—*The New York Times*

"An exploration of growing up in the punk scene, getting sober, finding love, and how something as simple as eating hundreds of slices of pizza can be the catalyst for personal growth."

—*The A.V. Club*

"This is the kind of book I want to make a gift of to everyone I know—lost, found, gluten-intolerant, cheeseheads. Heck, all of them need to read this! Everyone has something to gain from this tale of blackouts, almost burning out and too-burned crusts."

—*Newsweek*

"A powerful, unique blend of a better-late-than-never coming-of-age story and account of a recovering that is both involving and affecting . . . *Slice Harvester* deftly outgrows the high concept nature of its roots and delivers something altogether winning, the perfect balance of crust, cheese and sauce, exactly what a reader craves."

—*Toronto Star*

"Hagendorf's popular Slice Harvester blog chronicled his quest to eat and review a slice of cheese pizza from every pizzeria in Manhattan. In this entertaining memoir, he mashes up that journey with the topics of addiction, family, punk rock, nostalgia, and love . . . Full of drinking binges, colorful characters from the punk scene, and random asides, like comparing a slice to Anthony Kiedis, the narrative takes readers on a roller-coaster ride."

—*Publishers Weekly*

"*Slice Harvester* by Colin Atrophy Hagendorf is a must read for every New Yorker, city visitor, and/or pizza lover . . . Replete with detail, sarcasm, and poignancy, this 'memoir in pizza' is (perhaps surprisingly) the furthest thing from trivial."

—*Flavorwire*

"Colin's memoir is a rare story, both funny and heavy, using his trajectory as pizza blogger/zinester to pick apart his own self growth, and also channel a social and political subtext you would expect from someone raised on a critical punk worldview."

—*The Media*

A Memoir in Pizza

SLICE HARVESTER

Colin Atrophy Hagendorf

SIMON & SCHUSTER PAPERBACKS

New York London Toronto Sydney New Delhi

Simon & Schuster Paperbacks
An Imprint of Simon & Schuster, Inc.
1230 Avenue of the Americas
New York, NY 10020

Note to readers: Some names and identifying characteristics of people portrayed in this book have been changed.

First Simon & Schuster paperback edition November 2016

SIMON & SCHUSTER PAPERBACKS and colophon are registered trademarks of Simon & Schuster, Inc.

For information about special discounts for bulk purchases, please contact Simon & Schuster Special Sales at 1-866-506-1949 or business@simonandschuster.com.

The Simon & Schuster Speakers Bureau can bring authors to your live event. For more information or to book an event, contact the Simon & Schuster Speakers Bureau at 1-866-248-3049 or visit our website at www.simonspeakers.com.

Interior design by Ruth Lee-Mui
Illustrations by Joe Porter

Manufactured in the United States of America

10 9 8 7 6 5 4 3 2 1

The Library of Congress has cataloged the hardcover edition as follows:

Hagendorf, Colin Atrophy.

Slice harvester : a memoir in pizza / Colin Atrophy Hagendorf.
    pages cm
1. Hagendorf, Colin Atrophy.   2. Food writers—New York (State)—New York—
Biography.   3. Hagendorf, Colin Atrophy—Blogs.   4. Pizza—New York (State)—New
York.   5. Hagendorf, Colin Atrophy—Relations with women.   6. Young men—
New York (State)—New York—Biography.   7. Alcoholics—New York (State)—New
York—Biography.   8. Self-actualization (Psychology)   9. New York (N.Y.)—
Biography.   I. Title.
    CT275.H2514A3 2015
    974.7'1044092—dc23
    [B]
                                                                                              2014046048

ISBN 978-1-4767-0588-0
ISBN 978-1-4767-9054-1 (pbk)
ISBN 978-1-4767-0589-7 (ebook)

This book is for
Scott Hagendorf and Jamie Ewing

SLICE HARVESTER

On August 11, 2009, I set out to eat a plain slice from every pizzeria in Manhattan.

On November 22, 2011, two years and 435 slices later, I ate the last one.

This is my story.

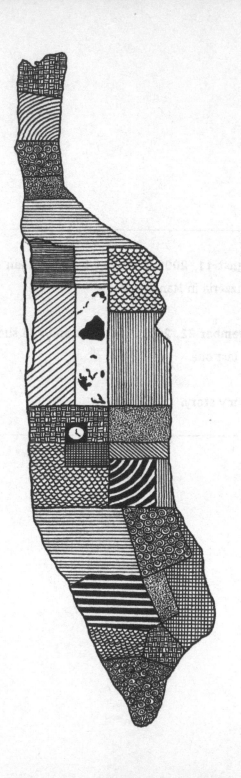

PROLOGUE

Less than a dozen blocks from the very tip-top of the island of Manhattan sits Grandpa's Brick Oven Pizza, its oddly tropical facade a bright orange contrast to the drab surrounding buildings. There's a fake wooden awning, the whole place is painted the color of an underripe clementine, and in the summertime the Italian ice cart stationed out front sports one of those grass umbrellas. Imagine if Tom Hanks built a pizzeria on the island he was stuck on in that movie I've never seen where he talks to a volleyball. That's kind of what Grandpa's looks like.

The fact that the very first stop on my pizza-eating odyssey looked more like a tiki hut than a pizzeria was either auspicious or ominous, I couldn't tell which—or maybe I was too hungover to care. But either way, I felt a vague sense of anxiety standing outside, knowing that if I stepped through the door and ordered a slice of pizza, I was committing to something big—and taking my plans out of the realm of Drinking and Talking and into the realm of Going and Doing.

Not that Drinking and Talking is a bad place to be—tons of

the best unshot films, unpainted murals, unillustrated graphic novels, and unrecorded music live together in the land of Drinking and Talking. They lead happy-go-lucky lives inside their consequence-free bubble. If you take a look inside, it's like peering through the window of the Barbie Dreamhouse at Barbie and Ken cooking some vegan chili while Skipper and Midge collate zines in the living room: the residents of Drinking and Talking are all perfect, fully realized, flawless. But as soon as you try to coax one of them into the world of Going and Doing, you realize that their legs don't bend the right way and their heads pop off if you're not careful. What I'm trying to say is, Drinking and Talking is much safer than Going and Doing.

That's what I was thinking about while looking in the window of Grandpa's Pizza. A few weeks ago it seemed so easy. I was drinking wine with a buddy of mine and said I was gonna eat a plain slice from every pizzeria in New York City. I was gonna eat *all the pizza*. How had no one done that yet? 'Cause I was gonna do it! I'd call myself the Slice Harvester, like some kind of mozzarella-fueled superhero. Best idea I'd ever had.

A few weeks passed. I continued riding my bike around delivering food, drinking with my friends, going to punk shows. I told everybody about my great idea (I didn't have to take it out of Drinking and Talking to do that, since we were all always drunk). One night while doing speed with my friend Sweet Tooth and listening to the contents of this suitcase full of cassette tapes he'd found in the trash, I said, "Listen, I've got it. I'll start at the top of Manhattan and go down, west to east, until I get to the bottom. That's how I'm gonna do it. Start at the top, work my way down."

Tooth was intently respooling one of the cassette tapes; he didn't even look up, just monotoned, "When do we start?"

"I don't know," I said. "I work all weekend. What are you doing Tuesday?"

And that's how on Tuesday evening, August 11, 2009, I wound up standing outside Grandpa's Brick Oven Pizza with a composition notebook and a pen I'd bought at the dollar store, wondering whether I had the chutzpah to follow through.

At least that's what I thought I was feeling, based on the nausea, but it may have just been that I was hungover and hadn't consumed anything all day except bodega coffee and the shittiest cigarettes—the best I could afford on my delivery-boy wages (not that I'm complaining). I'd spent that afternoon guzzling weak coffee at the copy shop, printing up zines for Support New York, the survivor support collective my best friend Milo and I had been part of for almost a decade. The collective was getting ready to host a table at some conference or anarchist book fair, and because I'm an eternal procrastinator, I ended up schlepping this granny cart full of zines along on my inaugural pizza mission.

Maybe I was nervous *and* hungover; it doesn't matter. What matters is that eventually I tilted back my cart and pushed it through the door.

Grandpa's is just as ultraorange and oddly tropical on the inside as its exterior implies. There were quite a few customers on line ahead of me. I couldn't really make out what any of them were saying over the Trio Reynoso record blaring from behind the counter, but there were two definitely stoned construction workers in front of me who seemed hella stoked for the pizza, and their excitement was infectious. I took it as a good sign, too, because in my experience, carpenters and electricians work all over the city and tend to know where the good food is.

When it was my turn I intoned, "Gimme a regular slice" (because that's how you say it in New York—none of this fa-kakta "Pardon me, sir, I'd like one piece of cheese pizza, please," okay?), and headed to my table, which was also orange and was decorated with what looked like crayon drawings of lighthouses and other Beach Shit that in no way made Grandpa's resemble a tropical paradise.

I'd like to say I savored that first slice, but the truth is I slammed it in, like, one minute flat. See, the slice at Grandpa's is too thin to support its own weight, and not good enough to be worth how little food you get for your money ($2.50 in 2009, $2.75 in 2014). I crammed probably half the slice in my mouth on my first bite. Admittedly, I'm really good at cramming things into my mouth, but even an amateur could've wrecked this flimsy pizza.

Still, even in my hungover haze, I knew there was more to Grandpa's slice than its lack of structural integrity. Despite being too small, the flavors were all totally right on—the cheese tasted like cheese, not like chemicals; the sauce was slightly sweet and slightly tangy; the dough was salty enough—but the ratios were off. There was a decent amount of sauce and cheese, but there wasn't enough dough to support it. Pizza is a food that you're supposed to be able to eat while you walk, and this slice would've been far too sloppy for that. What's a guy in a rush sup-posed to do? If I had tried to eat this on the go, I would've splat-tered tomato sauce all over my Crass tank top. Good ingredients, good flavor, bad ratios, too much money. This was basically right in the middle of good and bad. Completely neutral.

I jotted all these thoughts down in my new notebook, along with the name and address of the pizza place. Maybe it's hindsight, but I feel like a slice with some ideal qualities and some obvious flaws was the perfect way to start my career as a pizza reviewer. It would now be up to me to travel across the island of Manhattan to sift through all the complexities of the various combinations of cheese and sauce and the nuances of crust, flavor, bite, ratios, and aftertaste in search of the perfect slice, and to warn my fellow citizens against inferior pizza. I grabbed my cart and headed out the door.

The Slice Harvester was born.

CHAPTER 1

> ## Pizza Delia
>
>
>
> Majorly undercooked; this slice hung like a limp dick when I folded it. The dough and the sauce were both *way* too sweet, and the slice itself was unpleasantly heavy. I could tell with each bite that it was gonna sit in my gut like a brick. I started to bemoan the fact that Sweet Tooth wasn't around to help me finish it, because I can't stand to waste food. I begrudgingly made it to the crust, which was totally awful—undercooked, but still dense. When I left I actually kicked a telephone pole and muttered, "Fuck that place," under my breath.
>
> —*Slice Harvester Quarterly*, Issue 1,
> "Uptown," visited on August 12, 2009

Opposite page: The author, St. Marks Pizza

I **grew up** in a banal, bland, boring, busted-ass suburb.

Okay, it wasn't actually *that* bad. It was maybe even pretty cool, as suburbs go. But saying "I grew up in a pretty cool, ethnically and economically diverse city that seemed paltry in the shadow of New York but would be a huge cultural metropolis in Montana or Tennessee" doesn't really contain the same dramatic tension.

When I became a teenager and could get into the City on my own, I would go whenever possible. I wanted out of my circumscribed suburban existence, ASAP. I wanted to role-play another life—a feeling I imagine is universal in adolescents, at least among former overachievers with greaseball aspirations. And via a ride on a commuter train that lasted just long enough to polish off a forty of Old English, which had taken at least an hour of shoulder-tapping men outside the gas station to acquire, I could be transported into another world. The destination was always somewhere around St. Marks Place, located in the once-interesting East Village, the Colonial Williamsburg of kids from the suburbs who pretended to be kids from the City.

I was in its thrall for the wild youth culture and the easy

access to cigarettes and beer (which, for a fifteen-year-old, exercised the attraction of a tractor beam), but I also felt the gravitational pull toward St. Marks for its food. Coney Island High was great, and all those T-shirt shops and gangs of teenagers were really cool, too. But tacos at San Loco! My first ever falafel! Tofu and ginger dressing at Dojo! Burgers at Paul's! By far two places I frequented most were Ray's Pizza Bagel Cafe and St. Marks Pizza.

I went to Ray's pretty much exclusively for the everything bagels. For whatever reason, I was far more drawn to the pies across the street at St. Marks Pizza. My friends all thought I was crazy, because the slice at Ray's was bigger and cost less—by fifty cents, maybe. Fifty cents constituted one-half the price of a forty of Hurricane back then, so it was a lot of money in some respects, but to me, it was always worth it to spend the extra two quarters and splurge on a slice at St. Marks; it was so much better.

Perhaps because it's been closed for ten years now and there can be no going back to double-check my memory, St. Marks Pizza is my Pie in the Sky. It is the slice of nostalgia that every piece of pizza I've eaten since has fallen short of. The pizza was good, damn good; this fact has been corroborated by countless other nostalgists I've met. But my memory of the pizza there is colored just as much by my teenage perceptions (and delusions) of the world that St. Marks and its constituents opened up to me.

I ate at St. Marks Pizza the first time I ever set foot on the block. I was thirteen years old, languishing in the barren cultural wasteland that is Adolescence in the Suburbs, and had just read my first issue of *Maximum RocknRoll** thanks to a shout-out on the first page of *Spin* magazine. Shortly after I saw it in *Spin*, I was in Tower Records with my dad while he was buying some new Miles Davis remaster or something and spotted the zine's flat, newsprint form on the magazine rack. By its glaring lack of effort to entice me, it stood out among the glossy music and tattoo magazines. It almost looked like it was trying to *dissuade* potential readers rather than draw them in. I was smitten, and the universe decided: I would be a punk.

Sometime after reading that first issue of *MRR* I heard about St. Marks Place (or just "St. Marks," if you're not an asshole), I'm not sure where or from whom. I didn't even understand that it was a street named "St. Marks Place"—I just knew it was a location, and I knew it was where I belonged. And at the end of that summer it became apparent that I would need, more than anything, a pair of awesome combat boots in order to officially be punk. And I knew I had to go to Trash and Vaudeville on St. Marks to get them.

I don't know where I got these notions. This was before the ubiquity of the internet, so I wasn't exposed to new culture online. Most of my ideas about what being a punk meant were cribbed from Rancid videos on MTV or pictures of the Clash I had seen on albums in my parents' record collection. Regardless of where in the cultural ether I had drawn my notion that Combat Boots = Punk Legitimacy from, it was something I knew to be incontrovertibly true.

**Maximum Rocknroll*, or *MRR*, is the longest-running monthly punk fanzine in America, published since 1982. It got kind of dumb for a few years, but lately, via a series of Rad Women coming on as coordinators, it has become So Fucking Cool again.

Plus, I had gotten a pair of fake-leather knockoff Dr. Martens for next to nothing at Caldor at some point, but they were stupid and made my feet sweat and weren't tough enough.

So I did the only thing that made sense to me: I asked my dad to take me to St. Marks to buy boots. I don't think it even crossed my mind that I might have gone there unattended, even though by 1996 I had spent a fair amount of time in the Meatpacking District and the West Village, visiting my dad's younger brother and his girlfriend at their various apartments. I felt at home in downtown Manhattan and knew the lay of the land, or so I thought. But St. Marks, by then already well on its way to being the gentrified playground it is today, was like a jungle to me—so fierce, so real. I was scared by it, but I wanted in. I wanted to feel comfortable there. I wanted to be part of the scenery that both scared and lured the next suburban kid to step foot on the block.

Before attempting to acquire new boots, my father and I went to Paul's on Second Avenue to get a couple of burgers so as not to shop on an empty stomach. The burgers from Paul's were good, affordable and filling, as they have always been and shall always be. We set off down St. Marks with full stomachs, content, ready to find me the freshest combat boots in history. First stop: Trash and Vaudeville.

Trash and Vaudeville has been capitalizing on teenagers' desire to spend their parents' money on comically stupid clothes since the mid-seventies. Upstairs is the clothing store, which we wandered into by accident. It is a cavernous space, full of expensive Punk Couture, the legacy of Malcolm McLaren and Vivienne Westwood's Sex boutique. It was here that I saw my first pair of bondage pants, a far cry from my superbaggy JNCO jeans, which at the time I thought were the beginning and end of fashion. I also remember seeing a purple velour dinner jacket with a leopard-print lapel and matching leopard tuxedo pants and silently promising myself, *I will wear that to my prom* (a promise that remains unfulfilled, mostly because I didn't go to my prom).

But bondage pants and dinner jackets were just fanciful distractions from the task at hand: the acquisition of tough boots, of which, to my dismay, there seemed to be none in inventory. My father questioned the aging clerk, from whom I would, years later, receive a discount on a pair of stretch jeans in exchange for letting him watch me change. He informed us that there was a separate shoe store in the basement and that we had to exit the store and reenter from the street in order to gain access to it. As we left, I made a mental note to get my whole wardrobe from this place as soon as I was a grown-up.

Downstairs at Trash and Vaudeville is a scene. The walls are covered in decades' worth of graffiti and stickers; there is a glass counter running along the west wall filled with band patches, buttons, spikes, studs, and weird Goth jewelry; and there are shelves and shelves of subculturally relevant shoes. There were big space sneakers for ravers, winklepickers for mods, brothel creepers for rudies, and, of course, boots (*Boots!*) for the punks and skins. I skimmed the wall, pointing out pairs to my father that I thought were cool. He looked skeptically at the price tags and hurried me out of the store.

We walked together up the street. I was sad, but trusting. My father is a man of the world, and he seemed to have purpose. "This place looks cool, Colin, but it's a rip-off. This street is where everyone comes to buy combat boots. What we need to do is, we need to find the store where no one goes to buy combat boots." I think I looked a little crestfallen, because he added, "Let's walk around a little, and if we don't find anything, we'll come back." (Spoiler alert: we eventually found the exact same boots for, like, $50 less in the faaaaar West Village.)

We set out west on St. Marks, our bellies still full of burgers. We got to the corner of Third Avenue, and though I had never been there before, I recognized this as the border of my newfound homeland. As we crossed the avenue, my father and I both stopped dead in our tracks in the middle of the street and turned our heads back to the eastern sidewalk. A wisp of smoke had unfurled from an open storefront window, taken the shape of a human hand, and was beckoning to us with a come-hither finger.

I looked up at my father. "Do you smell that?"

"Pizza," he said, his eyes gleaming.

"Those burgers were pretty big, Dad. I don't know if I'm hungry."

"Me, either, but we'll split a slice. This smells too good to pass up."

And so we turned tail and headed back to the corner, where St. Marks Pizza sang its siren song.

We waited for our pizza with bated breath. I don't remember if the pizza shop was crowded or empty, I don't remember what the guy behind the counter looked like, I just remember a feeling of intense anticipation. It trumped my burning but childish desire for boots. All of my consciousness was fixated on the forthcoming slice.

When the pizza arrived, shining with oil, I was so excited that I picked it up with two hands.

"Hold on!" my father said urgently and slapped the slice down to the counter. "Only assholes eat pizza like that. Here, let me show you."

He took the slice in one hand and placed his index finger on the center of the top of the crust, with his middle finger and thumb beneath either side. "Listen carefully," he said as he pushed the two sides up along the fulcrum of his finger, folding the slice perfectly in half. There was an audible crackling as the crispy bottom shattered along the seam.

"Real New Yorkers fold their slices in half. Do it like this, or people might think you're a tourist." He handed me the folded slice so that I could take the ceremonial first bite.

It was perfect. Warm, but not so hot that it burned my mouth. The crust was crisp on the bottom, the sauce spiced just so, the cheese supple and delicious. And the smell! From that pizzeria emanated a delectable odor that was once far more common in New York. Today it reminds me of simpler times, because I was a teenager then, and everything was simpler when I was a teenager.

Despite eating pizza at least once a week growing up, the slice I had at St. Marks Pizza that day with my father stands out in my memory as the first perfect slice I ever had. The second came in my early twenties, on Broadway in Brooklyn, when I was on my way to the first show I ever saw at the Bent Haus, a ramshackle building on Bartlett Street that hosted raucous punk shows for many years. Local party punks Bent Outta Shape lived there, and my new friend Kevers had invited me to the show. I was excited to see the bands and nervous at the prospect of having to make new friends. I had just moved into an apartment on Lorimer Street, so it must've been almost 2004 or 2005. Walking down the hill toward Broadway, slurping a Ballantine tallboy out of a paper bag, I was brimming with both unfettered excitement and crippling social anxiety, mitigated only slightly by my malt liquor buzz.

It's fitting that I can vividly remember the slice of pizza I ate before the show, but the bands I was so excited to see are now a mystery to me. (Was it JRR Tallcan? Could it have been MTAnus?) I do know that it was around Halloween and I was dressed in a child-sized, polyester Hulk Hogan costume that I had cut into two pieces and was wearing as a midriff shirt–capri pants combo over a set of dollar-store long johns. I had a fake mustache I'd spray-painted yellow and glued to my face while it was still wet, so I was more or less constantly huffing glue and paint the whole night.

I was a little drunk, but the autumn air chilled my body through my scanty attire. I turned the corner onto Broadway, a street I had spent little time on but whose elevated train tracks and bustling sidewalk culture reminded me of Jamaica Avenue in Queens, near my grandmother's house. I shivered as I stepped into the shade of the tracks, and hoped the house wasn't too far away. Consulting the directions scribbled on the back of my hand proved unhelpful. As I walked down Broadway, I caught that smell again, the one that has followed me my whole life—a smell that lingered on that block so strongly that it overcame the paint fumes from the mustache right under my nose. Sure enough, a few storefronts past the Crown Fried Chicken was a pizza shop with its window open to the street.

I bought a slice and ate it as I walked the remaining blocks, which suddenly seemed shorter. It was delicious, that piece of pizza. It was on the wet side of the perfect ratio, but it had that special, intangible something that makes a slice terrific. I was a little bit tipsy and a big bit nervous about going to the show; my insides flickered like TV static, and I felt lighter than air, as if a gust of wind might send me tumbling down the street. But that slice of pizza solidified me. Its warmth spread from my belly all the way out to my limbs, and suddenly I was back in my body, ready for action.

I've been back to that place dozens of times in the decade since that day, and it's always a decent slice, but it's never been that good again. That particular evening I wasn't just eating a slice of pizza, I was eating all of the endless possibilities of youth. I was eating all of my hopes and dreams, and the thrilling sense of excitement that accompanied my fears. And let me tell you, a slice of pizza flavored with boundless innocence tastes great.

Looking back, I can see that both of my favorite slices symbolize benchmark moments in my development. That slice on St. Marks Place with my father when I was thirteen was the end of my childhood. That day was probably the last time we genuinely enjoyed each other's company for many years. Shortly thereafter I hit my sullen teenagehood and disavowed my awesome and loving family in an effort to establish my independence in the world. I cast myself off from the shores of familial love and was adrift at sea for quite some time, trying on different identities. And that slice on Broadway marks the end of those wanderings. I had found the Punx. I had found my way home.

There's this street character we used to always see in Tompkins Square Park back then who we called Screamin' Jesus. He was Frankenstein tall and had a big beard. He seemed to always be barefoot, sometimes draped in an American flag. He'd circle the perimeter of the park all day long, screaming, "BRITNEY SPEARS IS TURNING OUR DAUGHTERS INTO WHORES!" or "THE ROLLING STONES MADE MOMMIES AND DADDIES INTO SEX OBJECTS! MOMMIES AND DADDIES WEREN'T MEANT TO BE SEX OBJECTS!" All the young punks, in our merciless exuberance, would make fun of him. Not to his face, of course, because no one ever actually spoke to him. But on any given day one of us might take our boots off and stamp around in circles shouting nonsense in our best Screamin' Jesus impersonation.

I'm not sure when I first had a real conversation with him, but for a few years, whenever I saw him while I was working my delivery job, I'd stop frantically biking and he'd stop maniacally shouting and we'd talk briefly before both continuing on our respective, crazed ways. One afternoon I was talking with a friend when Screamin' Jesus walked by. I waved hello, and he jogged up to me, incredibly excited. "Hey, Colin!" he breathlessly began. "I don't know if you realize this, but every moment we have is a moment that's already passed us by. They're so quick and fleeting that we can't even hold them, and that might make you feel lost, but it's actually beautiful. You and I just had millions of moments together, Colin. Millions of moments in a span of seconds." And then he was off, berating a portly, sunbathing yuppie, "LOOK AT YOU, WITH YOUR EXPOSED NIPPLES AND YOUR FAT BELLY BESIDE . . ."

I think Screamin' Jesus summarized all the joy and pain of my young adulthood in that brief encounter. Since then that community has changed; I've changed. People have left town, dropped out of punk, passed away. Of the dozens of friends at that Halloween show, there's only a handful I still speak to on a regular basis, and only one I actually see more than a few times a year. None of those bands are still around, that's certain. We didn't expect any of them to endure for long. We were living in the end times. We didn't have to build things to last.

I guess it makes sense that what would prove to be the defining creative endeavor of my adult life would focus on the plain slice. On Day One of Slice Harvesting, I continued south from Grandpa's along Broadway. Sweet Tooth hadn't shown up, so I had some time alone to perfect my routine: Photograph the front of the pizzeria. "Lemmegetta regular slice." Photograph the slice. Eat. Furiously take notes. On to the next.

By this point I'd known Tooth for a few years. Sometime in the early 2000s some friends of mine were passing through New Orleans and met him on the street. They invited him to stay on their couch for a bit if he ever made it to Brooklyn, and he took them up on the offer about six months later, eventually living in that house for two years. He's been in and out of the city ever since. Sometimes it seems like he knows every punk in America. He may or may not have a nose ring (I can't remember), but he would definitely look good with one. His hair is always wildly unkempt and often dyed some odd color. He has homemade tattoos all over his arms and hands—most notably a crudely drawn rectangle on his left forearm, in which is written, "THE FUTURE IS A MACHINE AND YOU ARE SHIT."

Sweet Tooth's real name is Daniel, and he's a nice Jewish boy from Little Rock, Arkansas, though he set off across the roads and highways of America when he was fairly young. He ran an underground cinema in Oakland and a speakeasy rock club in Minneapolis. He recorded some of the weirdest and most beautiful music I have ever heard. He and I played together in a band called Nasty Intentions, once upon a time. It was probably the most fun band I've ever been in, but we kind of fizzled out, as punk bands often do, when half the group (Tooth included) moved away.

I liked Sweet Tooth immediately upon knowing him. We were kindred spirits. Anytime I got a weird new record, he was down to listen. Anytime he made ether from starter fluid, I was down to huff. We both felt an absolute and unwavering connection to Being Punk and the punk community at large, but we also had an interest in avant-garde art and music rooted in our teenage years and the influence of our strange fathers. How many other punks could I talk for hours about Sun Ra with while passing a bottle of poppers back and forth? Probably quite a few, actually, though for the purposes of this story, Sweet Tooth is the only one in the world.

I can say with absolute certainty that I wouldn't have been Slice Harvesting that day if it weren't for Sweet Tooth's half-assed encouragement, and I can speculate, as one is apt to do, that if I hadn't started Slice Harvesting *that day*, I may never have started at all; the Slice Harvester project may have remained for an idyllic eternity in the land of Drinking and Talking. So, in a sense, it is because of Sweet Tooth that you're reading this book. In short: this is all his fault. Curse him if you wish, but more important, if you are a pizzeria owner feeling maligned and litigious—Tooth is the guy to sue, not me.

That first day I wanted to sue Sweet Tooth for negligence myself. He had abandoned me. At first the solitude was pleasant, helping me hone my technique in peace, but five crummy slices in I needed some moral support. I lingered outside the sixth pizza place, Tony's, a little longer than usual, hoping I'd spot my buddy loping down the street.

Aesthetically the place was great, a picturesque hole-in-the-wall where a perfectly disheveled old man in a promotional Guitar Hero baseball cap served me a mediocre slice. I liked the man behind the counter. I wanted to like this place, too, but the slice was disappointing, and somehow that made my whole life seem disappointing, as a bad slice often can. Maybe it was just my lingering hangover, but I ate my terrible slice of pizza masochistically, as if each bite was penance for being such a worthless piece of shit. But suddenly Sweet Tooth came bursting through the door, dripping water everywhere, despite the fact that it didn't seem to be raining out. His eyes were darting back and forth and he was blinking like a mole man.

"I'm sorry I'm so late, Colin."

"Don't worry, Tooth. Why are you so . . . never mind. Are you okay?"

"You wouldn't believe what's been happening today. I woke

up and went out to Rockaway Beach and lost my glasses in the
ocean. I spent hours looking for them but couldn't see anything,
and no one helped me. I finally stumbled my way to the train
and got on and was on the way, and then all of a sudden the
train ground to a halt and the car started to fill with smoke because of a fire in the tunnel. They said it was caused by garbage
on the tracks, but everyone thought it was a terrorist attack or
something and started freaking out. Eventually we were all evac-
uated and I got onto a new train and made it up here, but you
weren't on the corner because it was so late, so I started going
into every pizzeria I could find, but I still couldn't see anything,
so I'd go up really close to people to see if they were you, and
then they weren't you and then I'd ask the people working if
they'd seen you and none of them remembered, and now I finally
found you and I'm sorry I'm late." He leaned in and hugged me
tight and soggy, out of breath from talking so fast.

"It's okay, buddy. Don't worry. Everything's okay now." I
wasn't only reassuring Tooth. "Let's go to the next place."

As we walked and talked, guided by a map I had drawn,
Pizza Palace, our final destination, loomed ahead. I started to
have my first doubts about the worthiness of this endeavor. Six
pizzerias in, and not only had I not had a single great slice yet,
I'd had five terrible slices. I wasn't feeling hopeful as Tooth and
I looked across Dyckman Street at an awning that read "PIZZA
* HEROES," presumably advertising slices and sandwiches, al-
though the proper pluralization of "hero" (the sandwich) would
be "heros." Tooth noticed the typo, turned to me, and muttered,
"You're my pizza hero."

From across the darkening street, I could see figures in the pizza parlor window—swarthy white men wearing red striped shirts, aprons, and paper hats giving daps to two Dominican teenagers wearing baggy tall tees and Bone Thugs braids. I could hear the strains of a Katy Perry song echoing from a tinny boom box. And I could imagine the exact scene playing out year after year, with different music coming from the boom box and different clothes and hairstyles on the teenagers. In my daydreams, Pizza Palace and its employees remain constant. I want to say that when we stepped into Pizza Palace it felt like we had stepped into a time machine, but it would be more apt to say that we had stepped *outside* of time. Pizza Palace is a magical space. It seems as if it has existed in one form or another since the Old Gods roamed the earth.

When we got inside, we noticed that there were three dudes behind the counter, all seemingly related and ranging in age from Probably, Like, Seventeen to John Turturro to Hella Old. We ordered our slice from Turturro, paid our money to Seventeen, and were eyed suspiciously by Hella Old. The slice itself was a mess—totally asymmetric, thicker than I usually like, a crust that looked like it had barely been in the oven, and cheese bubbling off the sides like hot lava. We got to the table, and before I even took a bite I said to my companion, "I'm afraid of this slice, Tooth."

He gave me the High Brow, a questioning glance.

"It's just . . . this place is so cool, and I really want the slice to be good. Plus, I'm honestly scared that if I say anything bad about it and one of the other customers or, god forbid, those guys behind the counter overhear me, they'll kick my ass! These people all seem like they take this pizza very seriously. It's a lot of pressure."

Tooth looked me dead in my eyes and said, "Colin, some-times fear is a key ingredient to a perfect slice." Truer words.

Luckily, we didn't have to find out what would have hap-pened if we talked shit about the pizza, because it was really good. It was different than I usually like, and was definitely not my ideal slice, but *damn, son*. It was so big I could barely fit the thing in my mouth. And it was wet, but not so wet that it was slipping and sliding all over the place—just wet enough. And just warm enough. This slice was big, wet, and warm. I wanted it in my mouth forever.

Things were looking up.

CHAPTER 2

Pizza Palace

They're obviously confident their pizza is good, because it looks sloppy as fuck, and they didn't even reheat it. This slice had thicker dough and more cheese than I generally prefer, but they were perfectly balanced so that every bite was a delight. And the dough was airy and fluffy, not dense and horrid. This really comes through in the crust, which, though it was thick and pale—two signs that it might be undercooked and crappy—had a nice crispness to it, and the inside was fluffy enough that it never felt overwhelming or heavy.

—*Slice Harvester Quarterly*, Issue 1,
"Uptown," visited on August 12, 2009

Opposite page: John Kambouris at his mixer

In order to fully understand the magic of Pizza Palace, we need to get to know John Kambouris, the man who has run the place for the past thirty years. Kambouris, who owns Pizza Palace with his brother, George, moved to New York City's Inwood neighborhood from Greece in the 1960s. He got a job as a dishwasher at a little restaurant on Broadway, then became a cook at a small diner in the Bronx, slowly crawling up the food-service food chain until 1971, when he opened his own coffee shop on Sherman Avenue. He ran that until 1986, when he bought Pizza Palace, which had originally been opened in 1945 by three brothers.

"They were guys from my home island," John told me in his slight Greek accent one afternoon when I stopped at Pizza Palace for a slice. "The three brothers, one of them wanted to leave. He said to me, 'John, what are you doing in this coffee shop? Buy my share of the pizza parlor. Pizza—this is where you will make your money.'

"'But what do I know of pizza?' I asked him. 'Pizza is easy,' he told me. 'I will teach you.' And so I thought this offer over, and I have been here ever since."

He punctuated this statement with a small stamp of his foot and a grand sweep of his arms around his pleasantly rundown pizza shop, smiling proudly.

Like any part of New York, Inwood is a neighborhood with a long and complex history. Inwood Hill Park is where Peter Minuit "purchased" Manhattan from the island's indigenous people. The Dutch began settling there in the seventeenth century, but the only traces of their former presence are the name of Dyckman Avenue and a Dutch Colonial farmhouse built in 1784 that's now a museum called the Dyckman House. And the projects in Inwood are known as the Dyckman Houses. A museum and a housing project are nearly polar opposites in terms of usage and public perception of value, so there is a certain unpleasant irony in the fact that these two spaces share a name.

The neighborhood remained relatively rural until the early twentieth century, when subways were built to connect it to the rest of the city and new construction began to flourish. Irish laborers were brought in to build apartment houses, which they subsequently moved into. The Irish were soon followed by a wave of Jewish immigrants fleeing the dreary claustrophobia of the Lower East Side, and a small enclave of Greeks (including John Kambouris) came over from Kos, a tiny island one-twentieth the size of Delaware, with a smaller population than that of Minot, North Dakota.

Inwood was pretty suburban until the late 1940s, when Robert Moses built the Dyckman Houses, a seven-building project on Tenth Avenue. This was also when two of the neighborhood's most famous residents were born: Kareem Abdul-Jabbar, who was born and raised in the Dyckman Houses and grew up to be really tall and also the highest-scoring basketball player ever, and writer/famous junkie Jim Carroll, although he didn't move to Inwood until he was fifteen. His most famous book, *The Basketball Diaries*, is about being a dirtbag teen here, though pretty much any New York neighborhood worth its salt has inspired some kind of art about being a dirtbag teen: Upper East Side: *The Catcher In the Rye*; Queensbridge: *The Infamous Mobb Deep*; Lower East Side: *Low Life* by Luc Sante; etc.

By the seventies, many of the Irish, Jewish, and Greek families had left, following the pattern of white flight exhibited in much of the city, and the neighborhood was settled by a wave of newcomers from the Dominican Republic, many of whom remain today. During the eighties, Inwood was hit hard by the crack epidemic and all its accompanying violence and desolation—which brings us to 1986, when John Kambouris bought Pizza Palace from his buddy from the Old Country.

During the next two decades, John saw the pizzeria he had taken over as one of the few constants in the otherwise unstable urban terrain of Inwood. Many of the Dominican residents who had come to the neighborhood as kids during the 1970s had grown up eating the pizza there, and began to bring in their children to sample the slices. Today there are at least three generations in the neighborhood who have eaten at Johnny's, as the place is locally known.

I asked John's son, Nick, a jovial guy about my age who at the time was studying for his master's in education but still helping out around the pizza shop on busy days, what he thought of the neighborhood and what had compelled his father to stay when the bulk of the Greek community left for Queens and the Bronx. "Even though the people have changed, the neighborhood is still the same: a stepping-stone for recent immigrants. Neighborhoods like this are important to the city, and our pizza shop ties the community that is currently here to the community that left. It gives people a reason to hold on to their identity. Inwood is a great place to keep your culture and traditions and learn what it means to be American at the same time."

This is why I love New York. The dense population and physical proximity to other humans from wildly disparate backgrounds forges bonds that would be hard to create elsewhere. And yet I often run into lifelong New Yorkers who seem to feel the exact opposite way. A couple of days ago, for instance, I was talking to a guy standing in line in front of me at a pizza parlor (another result of the close proximity of New Yorkers: people waiting in line together engage in light small talk, and it isn't weird), and he mentioned that he had grown up in Richmond Hill.

I said, "No shit! A bunch of my family lived there decades ago, and I've got a couple of friends who grew up there. Seems like an interesting neighborhood. It's mostly Caribbean and Indian these days, right?"

"Yeah," he said wistfully, shaking his head slowly back and forth and looking down at the counter. "It used to be Irish and Italian." He raised an eyebrow and looked at me as though I obviously understood and agreed with him that it should have stayed that way. What a nob!

My dad's family moved from Williamsburg, Brooklyn, to Rosedale, Queens, when he was still a kid. Rosedale is a suburban neighborhood just north of Kennedy Airport, right on the border of Queens and Long Island. When my dad was little, the neighborhood was mostly Jewish and Italian families like my father's—immigrant parents trying to inch their children out of the densely populated urban enclaves where they had initially settled, taking one incremental step closer to realizing the suburban American dream of a white picket fence and a sprawling lawn.

I spent a lot of Jewish holidays in Rosedale as a kid. My grandparents would take me to the park, and then we'd go to the Buttermill, a Jewish bakery that made the best mandel bread I've ever had, or to the Woodro delicatessen for knishes, pastrami sandwiches, and black cherry soda. My grandmother died when I was thirteen. When I was nineteen, my grandfather moved to Florida as part of the ongoing Great Jewish Migration. (All New York Jews, when they reach a certain age and if they have the means, move to Florida.)

But I still go to Rosedale at least once a year to visit my best friend's mother, Mrs. Watson, who came to New York from Jamaica thirty or forty years ago. As I observed to the Pizza-Line Bozo about Richmond Hill, Rosedale seems predominantly Caribbean these days—mostly Jamaican and Haitian, I think. When I visit with Mrs. Watson, instead of knishes and black cherry soda we eat beef patties and drink sorrel punch, but the feelings of love are the same. The kvetching is the same, though in a different dialect. The sense of pride in being able to own a home in a nice neighborhood is the same.

I began visiting Mrs. Watson a few years after my grandfather moved out of Queens. Returning to Rosedale, seeing the same landscape populated by different people, always seemed so beautiful to me. That a geographic location could serve the same function for multiple immigrant communities in succession always seemed like a tiny victory in a city full of tragedy. So when people like that shmuck at the pizza shop spew their xenophobic nostalgia, it really galls me. Part of me wanted to shout at the guy, but part of me wanted to talk to him nicely. In my daydreams I tell him, "You do realize, don't you, that back when that neighborhood was Irish, the Irish were scorned and quietly feared by mainstream white America in the same way you are looking down on your desi neighbors in Richmond Hill? You've only been white for, like, a hundred years! Get over yourself! And enjoy the slice. It's on me." Of course I didn't say any of that, because I don't usually lecture strangers, and I can't afford to buy their pizza. Or I'm a gutless coward. You decide.

In his two-part essay *Times Square Red, Times Square Blue,* Samuel Delany—Bronx native, award-winning science fiction writer, preeminent documentarian of cruising culture in New York City, my favorite author—writes that within the now nearly eradicated cruising scene in the porno theaters of Times Square, he saw more "cross-class contact" than in any other type of space in New York City. I would say that the Ideal Pizzeria shares this quality—though perhaps to a lesser extent—and that these characteristics are embodied perfectly by the scene at Pizza Palace on Dyckman Avenue.

Here we have first, second, and third generations from a handful of different nations preparing and eating food together: young mothers gossiping in Spanish with their strollers parked at the edge of the table; less-affluent Columbia students who can't afford the rents in Morningside Heights, and so settled in

Inwood; seemingly ageless neighborhood junkies who could be a world-worn thirty or a pickled, preserved seventy; young seminary students on their way back from visiting the Cloisters—all have a slice waiting for them. And in the midst of it all is John Kambouris, standing in the back room at his sixty-year-old industrial mixer, making the dough for tomorrow's pies. In the two hours I sat at Palace Pizza during my last visit, nearly everyone who came in took a moment to wave at John, and he addressed most of them by name.

And the community spirit emanating from Pizza Palace traverses not only ethnic boundaries but national borders as well. The week I ate my last slice in Manhattan (two and a half years after the day I stepped into Johnny's), I was written up in a couple of local papers, one of which published a list of my five favorite pizza parlors, Pizza Palace among them. A week later I was doing a vanity google (that's when you type your own name into Google—don't try to pretend you haven't done it and don't know what I'm talking about) when I found a result written in the Greek alphabet. I sent it to a high school friend who reads Greek, and he informed me that the article was about Pizza Palace making my top five. The local paper from Kambouris's home island was so proud that one of their own had been awarded such a hefty distinction (one of the five best pizza parlors in all of *New York City*!) that they had chosen to write a human-interest piece about it.

In essence, Kambouris's success as a pizza man didn't impact only the residents of his neighborhood, who routinely have their bellies warmed by his wonderful food. His influence spreads farther even than the Inwood Diaspora, some of whom stop at "Johnny's" on Dyckman first thing after landing in New York, before seeing their own families. No, the ripples of John's labor and dedication to his neighborhood and his craft reached all the way across the Atlantic to the remote Greek island where he was born. Because the thing is, John Kambouris doesn't just own a warm and inviting establishment—no easy task in itself—but that's chump stuff compared to John's other skill: making damn good pizza.

The night of my first pizza mission with Sweet Tooth, I set up a blog and posted all six reviews immediately. I e-mailed a couple of friends to tell them I had finally sold out for good and joined the internet. That evening I stayed in for the first time in months; I didn't even drink a single beer. I was exhausted from walking around all day and excited about having begun something so potentially awesome. My ultimate plan was to put everything out as a fanzine, but I was feeling too ecstatic to sit on it. I wanted an immediate response.

A few days later I had a couple of e-mails from strangers asking me when I would update again. My friend Kimya Dawson, who finally received the widespread acknowledgment and admiration she had long deserved after being featured on the sound track for the movie *Juno*, had linked to Slice Harvester on her blog, and about five hundred billion people had looked at it. Another friend of mine posted a link on the blog for the yuppie kitchen accoutrements store she worked at, which got picked up by *Slice*, which is probably the only financed pizza website. And the pizzarazzi swarmed.

Suddenly the dumb thing I was doing because of my pure

love of pizza was being paid attention to by hundreds, maybe thousands, of people. Luckily, I have long subscribed to the old Ludichrist adage that "most people are dicks"* (and I am notoriously oblivious to what's going on around me), so this sudden spotlight didn't make me feel self-conscious or concerned.

I did, however, realize that if I wanted to pursue this thing in a way that would be the most rewarding for everyone involved, it would behoove me not to publish six posts in one night and then maintain silence for the rest of the week. As usual, the things that would be common sense to most people don't come so easily to me. But I learned this particular lesson quickly and painlessly, so in subsequent weeks I went out to eat pizza one day a week, hit five to seven places, took copious notes, and updated the blog nearly every day.

Summer proceeded, and my life continued down its banal and abysmal path despite my newfound calling. I got drunk a lot, did my really punk DJ night with Marcia at the really punk bar, got scabies, ate a bunch of pizza (both on and off the clock), and worked my dumb burrito delivery job. My best friend since high school moved to California. Most days I wore my denim vest with no shirt underneath. (I probably looked like a crust-punk Aladdin.) I didn't shower much and I neglected my cats, but they're still alive today and so am I, so it's all water under the bridge, right?

By autumn I had gotten rid of my scabies, gone on a bunch

---

*Ludichrist's first release, *Immaculate Deception*, is perhaps my favorite slept-on NYHC album. The relevant lyrical excerpt: *Most! People! Are! Dicks! DICKS! DICKS! DICKS!* It is my firm belief that if, in the coming epoch, the poetic musings of Tommy Christ are not taught as canon in all high schools and universities, we, as a species, are fucked. FUCKED! FUCKED! FUCKED!

of awkward OkCupid dates, and not given up on Slice Harvester. At the end of September, a reporter from the *Daily News* accompanied me on a pizza mission. I had always assumed there would be a passing interest in me once I had *finished* eating all the pizza, but the fact that a huge New York newspaper was compelled to write about me so early in the project was astounding. I don't even think it was an especially slow news day, either, because the front page of the edition in which my article appeared (on page 3, no less) had a headline about some foiled terrorist plot in Queens. Admittedly, that was probably one of those foiled terrorist plots in which an FBI snitch goads some suggestible dude into buying fake bombs from another FBI snitch and then arrests him, thereby keeping white America safe from and terrified of brown dudes from the Middle East. Or South Asia. Or Jackson Heights; blah blah blah, even Obama's America is racist, fuck the police (except for Columbo), you get the drift.

But I digress. The point is, I'm a deadbeat punk rocker; I am not media savvy and I have next to no business acumen, yet somehow I had blundered my way into this publicity wonderland. I didn't have to do anything but eat a bunch of pizza and write about it, and suddenly people were interested in what I had to say? Works for me.

But as my online following grew, so did the tenacity of my critics. A few days after the *Daily News* article I received multiple comments on my review of Tony's, the place from my first week of Harvesting where the picturesquely shlubby pizza man in the Guitar Hero hat served me a mediocre slice. They were all anonymous, but they ranged in tone from "I think your [*sic*] wrong about this place" or "If Tony's wasn't for you, it wasn't for you" to "You don't know what good pizza is because your [*sic*] on crack" and "BLOW THIS!! 8==D" Okay guys, you got me—say what you will about the slice at Tony's, but any pizza place that gets half a dozen people defending it must have something going for it.

On the tails of my *Daily News* coverage, I did a bunch of weird radio interviews, including one with this douchey older guy who had me on his *Maniac in the Morning* commuter-talk show. We arranged via e-mail that they would call me at 5:45 a.m., but I totally didn't care about the interview and was still up drinking and snorting yak when they rang. Oops! The dude was a total jerk, though, so who cares? At one point he asked me how many pizza places there were in New York City, and I said, "I dunno, three thousand?"

And the dude, who talked like Lewis Black, said, "Three thousand? Where'd you get that number?"

So I told him, "I don't know. I think my friend Phil told me." Even though that wasn't true.

Dude was all, "Your *friend* Phil? What does he know?"

"Phil?! Phil doesn't know anything. Phil's a scumbag," I blurted out, because that was true, inasmuch as we were all a bunch of scumbags back then. The host was totally disgusted that I said the word "scumbag" on his dickhead radio show because old people are really bothered by that word, and anyway, it didn't end well. After that, in every interview I gave—and I gave a ton that month—whenever they would ask me if I had anything more to add, I'd say, "Phil Chapman is a scumbag. Print that. P-H-I-L C-H-A-P-M-A-N." And they always edited it out. It became a running joke, and I couldn't wait for it to make it into the book one day. But now that I have the chance, I just want to say that Phil Chapman isn't actually a scumbag. Phil Chapman is my friend, and he's a good guy.

October got off to a good start—I finished eating all the pizza above Central Park, the first good delineator. Had I owned a giant map of Manhattan, I could have blocked out a substantial quadrant at the top. That's forty-seven different slices of pizza in a little over six weeks. Of those forty-seven, six were great and eight were good, which means 30 percent, or almost a third, of the pizza I ate was above average. Those aren't such horrible results.

And the bad pizza, while miserable to masticate, was a joy to write about. Rapturous descriptions of delicious slices get old pretty quick, but thinking about new and more vivid ways to describe the myriad failures enabled me to be really playful with my writing in a way I hadn't been since my high school fanzine, which had been coming out much less frequently as the years went on. In retrospect, it's easy to see that this lack of a creative outlet probably fed into my spiraling doldrums. In essence, each one of these terrible slices helped to incrementally pull me out of my funk.

Here are my three favorite insults from that era of Harvesting:

> "The dough was so dry that I felt like a guy in a cowboy movie who's been stuck in the desert for a week with a mouth full of sand."

> "The pockmarked texture of the burnt cheese reminded me of James Woods's grimacing visage as he masturbated his new belly-vagina with a pistol in *Videodrome*."

"The cheese was this weird, solid mass that was thick and congealed. I feel like it could be used by a scrappy and industrious mouse as the sail of a tiny boat he's constructing to make his way out of the city and find his true love in a children's movie."

It felt like I was doing something with my life, like I might not be doomed to an eternity of working shitty jobs and sitting at the bar every night talking about what I hadn't done or what I was gonna do. I had opened the door to an eternity of working shitty jobs and then sitting at the bar every night talking about something cool I had *actually done*!

Mid-month I threw out the giant couch my old roommate and I had moved to my apartment on four skateboards five years prior and bought a love seat from the Ghost of Christmas Future. For real—I went to this lady's house and it was, like, so full of junk that we had to move all this furniture to get the couch through the door. She was waaaaaay east on Twenty-Ninth Street, and I got the feeling the neighborhood had gotten fancy around her while she clung tooth and nail to her rent-stabilized apartment.

After she buzzed me in and I walked up the eternal staircase, she was at the door, practically a million years old, with a cigarette in her mouth. If she were a slice, she'd be the slab from your favorite pizza shop that you froze to save for later sometime last year that's still in your freezer, persevering. "You're probably gonna have to move some shit around," she rasped. We walked into her apartment, and there were three different TVs and a radio all playing different things at full volume.

When we finally made our way through the junk, she gestured with her cigarette toward the couch, which was buried under piles of old magazines. "It's a good fuckin' couch. I'm sad to see it go, but you seem like a nice kid." She was right about one thing: it was a great couch. But I couldn't shake the fact that I had just witnessed my potential future.

My friend Jamie wrote this song called "Stray Dog Town." The song opens with one of the most vivid and evocative lyrics any of my friends have ever put to tape:

One day I'll be nothing but a sad and lonely old man
doing my dishes.

Toward the middle of the song he screams it a second time. It's a plaintive wail, full of youthful bravery in the face of impending doom. I remember sitting on the fire escape at Jamie's house, drinking a Ballantine forty and watching his band play through the living room window. Everyone turned their amps up way too loud back then, so if you wanted to actually *hear* the music (as opposed to *feel* the music, I guess, but that sounds too hippie-ish), you had to listen from outside. I can easily recall my view through that window of a room full of friends and Jamie screaming into a microphone that was wrapped in a T-shirt to prevent him from getting shocked. When they played "Stray Dog Town" I turned my gaze to the kitchen window and could practically see Jamie stooped at the sink fifty years down the line, bare chested, his jutting bones casting shadows in the stark light of the naked overhead bulb.

It was the exact opposite of what was going on at that

moment right in front of me: Jamie in the living room, surrounded by people he loved and who loved him, all singing along to his songs. Sitting on that fire escape, I felt like my forty was the only thing keeping me from floating away. Jamie and I always had an affinity for each other, because we both recognized that our bravado and extroversion masked a deeply held sense of dissatisfaction with ourselves. We both felt a similar distance from those around us, and we both found solace in getting wasted and going to shows. I can't speak for Jamie, but I know I drank myself silly back then because I was trying to blot out my constant inner monologue, as much as I thought it was fun or joyful or some affirmation of coolness and life.

The song continues:

> *walkin' around so desperate for somethin'*
> *but we're the patron saints of doin' absolutely nothin'*
> *'cept runnin' our bodies into the ground*
> *I been runnin' outta hope every night in this stray dog*
> *town*
> *and I don't wanna end up broke down*
> *like a van at the side of the road now*

Looking back, there's a terrifying sense of foreboding in Jamie's statement that he didn't want to ever grow old, see his body deteriorate and his life fall apart. He died the night Barack Obama was elected. A few days later I was at a funeral home on Long Island looking into a casket at my friend, buried in his I ♥ NY T-shirt, a pair of jeans, and his black canvas sneakers, twenty-five forever.

November 2009 marked the one-year anniversary of Jamie's death and two and a half months of Slice Harvesting. Looking back on it, 2009 seems like so much more than a year. It began in the shadow of Jamie's death and ended with my own creative resurrection. In a sense, everything I did that year (and everything I've done since then) was partially motivated by a need to assuage some sense of guilt I had for still being alive. My buddy died, and he used to make such awesome music and art, and here I am, Not Dead, and I'm, like, wandering around the country drinking different regional rotgut whiskeys? The gall.

By December I had started working on the first issue of *Slice Harvester Quarterly*, the print form of the Slice Harvester blog, which had always been a goal of mine. I had been publishing zines since my adolescence, and it was something I missed—the late nights drinking coffee and listening to overloved cassettes; accidentally gluing my finger to the inside of my nostril because I picked my nose while assembling masters with rubber cement; the stack of finished copies a tangible result of my labor. It wasn't until I started putting *Slice Harvester Quarterly* #1 together that I realized how sorely I'd missed it.

If you traveled back in time and ran into High School Me and told him that Adult Me would end up writing a popular blog, High School Me would've said, "What's a blog?" and then after you explained it to him he would've been elated, but not necessarily surprised. *However*, if you used that same time machine to travel back and tell Adult Me when he was just starting Slice Harvester that he was about to go eat pizza with the star of some of his favorite childhood movies, he wouldn't have ever believed you. But you would be right.

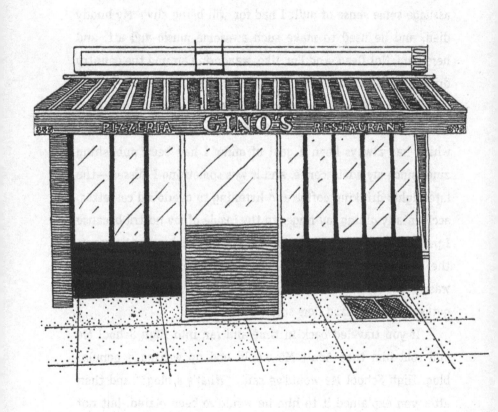

CHAPTER 3

Gino's

Crispy and charred on the bottom and cheesy on top, with a delicate sauce that you don't notice is there but would certainly miss if it were gone. Pizzerias like this are what make Slice Harvesting worth it.

—*Slice Harvester Quarterly*, Issue 3, "Upper East Side," visited on January 8, 2010

Opposite page: Gino's, 345 East Eighty-Third Street

Life was getting a little weird. In January 2010, I had been contacted via e-mail by a young lady named Greta, the high-school-aged daughter of Phoebe Cates—a genuine famous person!—who asked if the two of them could accompany me on some pizza eating. She had gotten my e-mail address through my friend Steve, whom she had gotten to know as a fan of his band No One and the Somebodies. I agreed to take her and her mother Slice Harvesting, for two reasons: eating pizza with a mother and her daughter sounded weird, and so did eating pizza with a movie star, and WHOA, what about doing both at once? Also, I'd eat pizza with anyone who was in *Drop Dead Fred*.

I invited my friend Caroline to come with us, because I can get a bit socially anxious sometimes and tend to make situations more difficult than they have to be; having Caroline along would provide the necessary buffer for hanging out with two potentially nonpunk strangers. At least if things got truly weird, she and I would be in it together.

The day of our celebrity meet-up arrived, and I was nervous. What if there was an unbridgeable gap between these people and me? A teenager and a grown-up! Both identities felt leagues away from where I was in my life. Like, I definitely was not a kid anymore, but I *definitely* was not a grown-up, either. I was living in that weird middle place—more than a girl, not yet a woman—of protracted adolescence that has maybe always existed but seems to me to be a first-world product of late capitalism in the early aughts, though this theory of mine is not even a little bit fleshed out. WHATEVER. I'm not Theodor Adorno, okay? Get over it.

When I got off the subway my phone buzzed in my pocket with a text from Greta that had come in while I was underground:

Chillin in gamestop

And I became truly scared.

We met on the corner and went to a pizzeria called Europan Pizza Cafe that I had been postponing because it looked crummy. Not, like, the decrepit or run-down kind of crummy—I like that kind of crummy. I'm talking about the kind of crummy that is too clean and polished to trust; the kind of crummy that has flat-screen TVs mounted in the walls, all playing the same looping video of a fireplace; the kind of crummy where Billy Joel is on the radio. I am hard-line anti-Joel. (There's some busted-ass trend in which New York punks have a soft spot for Billy Joel, and it needs to end. To paraphrase Abe Biotic: Fuck Billy Joel! Fuck your negative attitude! WE ARE THE PUNKS!)

When we got inside this terrible-looking place, Phoebs (*you* should still call her Phoebe) immediately began a conversation with the woman behind the counter as she ordered our slices.

As we were eating, she explained, "That woman used to work at my favorite pizza place in the neighborhood. It closed down, and a bunch of their employees came to work here." Any anxieties I had felt about my celebrity interaction were quelled—Phoebe was clearly fit to Harvest.

The pizza was surprisingly good—crispy and warm, with nice ratios and ingredients of decent quality. It was nothing amazing, but it was much better than I thought it would be from looking at the yuppie facade. I went through this whack phase in my life where I went on, like, eight hundred internet dates in a span of a few months. It was so stupid and unpleasant, and I am too much of a greasy weirdo for it to work for me. Ninety percent of the time I would meet people and know we weren't compatible within five minutes, but would finish the dates anyway out of some weird sense of masochism/manners; 7.5 percent of the people seemed cool at first but then turned out to be, like, subtly racist or something, and it was clear that it just wasn't worth it; and 0.5 percent of the people liked me and I liked them, and we went on another date. The leftover 2 percent were people I didn't vibe with romantically, socially, or culturally (and I just want to clarify here that when I say "culturally" I don't mean "people from India," I mean, like, ravers), but regardless of those differences we had a surprisingly good time together; it was a fun distraction and ended without any awkwardness or pretense. That's what this slice was like. It's always a pleasant surprise to have our prejudices put in check, to be reminded not to judge a person by their appearance or a slice by its storefront.

My social anxiety turned out to be unfounded. Phoebe did some heavy momming, which was awesome. She paid for everything, and made sure we all had enough root beer. She simultaneously treated the whole thing as if Caroline and I, twenty-nine and twenty-seven, respectively, were two kids on a playdate with her fifteen-year-old daughter, and also as if we were just four friends out to lunch—a tough line to walk. And I don't know whether I'm just out of touch with teenagers, but Greta was totally kind and charming and really bright, and it was a pleasure to spend an afternoon chatting with her.

At our fourth pizzeria—I think we were at the Upper East Side Two Boots, a place with weird pizza that I will always be nostalgic for because of the days when I used to eat for free at their Lower East Side shop—it finally occurred to me and Caroline that it was a little strange that we were hanging out with a teenager in the early afternoon on a weekday.

Phoebe was getting us a round of root beers, so it was just the three kids at the table when Caroline said, "Greta, what are you doing hanging out with a couple of near-thirty-year-olds at one p.m. on a Wednesday? Don't you go to school?"

Greta looked up from her slice and replied, "Nah, I get homeschooled. But it's bullshit; I don't do anything." Her face swelled with adolescent pride. Caroline and I noticed Phoebe strolling up with our drinks, definitely within earshot of Greta's proclamation.

"She's totally lying." Phoebe said as she sat down at the table and handed out drinks. "She's doing a photography class, she's taking Russian literature at CUNY, she does all kinds of stuff. She's even doing a riot grrrl band for an independent study." Phoebe was practically beaming as she said the last bit. "Tell them what it's called, dear."

Greta's face reddened, and she pouted a bit. "Period Farts," she said reluctantly.

It was the first time I'd seen her experience an emotion anywhere near embarrassment at something her mother had said. Which was jarring for me, because at fifteen, even being in the same room as either of my parents was cause to feel an acute sense of shame. I was embarrassed that they existed at all. For Caroline and me, this was a glimpse into a form of Cool Parenting that neither one of us had experienced. Not that my parents weren't kind or supportive or totally awesome—I mean, my dad gave me my first Dead Kennedys record—it's just that Cool Parenting takes a certain willingness on the part of the child to be parented that I just didn't have as a youngster because I was a selfish piece of shit.

In a sense, watching Greta's and Phoebe's ease and comfort around each other made me wish that I could go back and tell my teenage self what a dick I was being. I almost don't want to admit some of this stuff, because it makes me seem like a total ingrate, but like George Bush Jr. said when he was rescuing us from 9/11, "Let's roll."

When my high school punk band played our first show at CBGB, my parents *begged* me to let them come, and I absolutely refused. And what makes it worse, in retrospect, is that they respected my boundaries. Looking back, it's heartbreaking. I thought my friends were so lucky because their parents didn't have the slightest interest in anything we did. My parents infuriated me because they wanted to, like, I don't know, participate in my life a little, show an active interest in the things that interested me. And I flat-out shut them down every time.

Don't get me wrong: I understand where I was coming from.

Being a teenager is weird and hard, and the whole point is that you don't know all the stuff that you know when you're thirty. That's why it's so fun, but also why it sucks. Anyway, I guess my whole point is that my parents rule and I was a dick to them, and I want to take this opportunity to acknowledge that in front of everybody.

Okay, check this one out: Sometime around Thanksgiving when I was fifteen there was this huge show at 7 Willow Street, a cool punk club in Port Chester that I went to sometimes as a teenager. It was a Less Than Jake show, I think. I fought like hell (and lost) to get my dad to drop me off around the corner from this show, because I knew there would be a line outside the club and I didn't want other kids to see that I had parents. I didn't bring a jacket, because I knew it would be hot in there—and this was before smoking bans were everywhere, so there was literally no reason to go outside once the show started. As we pulled around the corner in front of the club, my father and I both noticed that a huge line had formed. I was chagrined at the notion of all of these people seeing me get out of his car; he was bothered by something else.

He said, "Why don't you let me wait in line and get your ticket for you? It's cold."

And I said, "You don't know anything. There's not a ticket—they just stamp your hand."

And he said, "Well, then borrow my jacket," which was one of those weird smooth leather jackets like the one Ross had on *Friends*.

I was all, "Ewww, no, I hate you, leave me alone," and got out of the car.

Something like fifteen minutes later I was halfway through

the line, which was the kind that snakes back and forth through velvet ropes so that a million people can get crammed into a dense yet organized square, and I noticed this jostling toward the back, but didn't pay it any mind. The commotion seemed to be advancing on me, but I didn't really care—and then all of a sudden there was my dad, standing in front of me, holding out a sweater he had taken from the trunk of his car.

"Here, just take this; I don't care if you lose it. It's so cold out here. This is ridiculous."

I pretended I didn't know him, and spoke through gritted teeth. "UGH! I *hate* you. I don't need a sweater. Go AWAY!"

And then he looked at me and said, "All right, see ya later, champ," and he gave me one of those playful little slo-mo punches on the chin like a coach gives a basketball player.

And I was livid. Livid, I tell you! That was the only time in recorded history that he ever called me "champ," and the only time he ever did one of those stupid chin punches. The whole show was ruined, because in the breaks between bands, when the different groups of kids would stand in circles and smoke cigarettes and joke around, anytime any of those little circular cells of my peers would erupt into laughter, I'd just imagine all the kids giving mock chin punches and sarcastically calling each other "champ" while pointing back at me and laughing.

But enough fraught moments from my otherwise idyllic childhood; back to the pizza.

When Phoebe, Greta, Caroline, and I left Two Boots, we made our way to a pizzeria called Fat Sal's, a fairly nondescript place, not especially bad or good aesthetically. The slice was so-so—inoffensive, if a bit weird. It had a decent texture and okay ratios, but an odd flavor. Caroline thought it tasted like shrimp ramen. That didn't especially perturb me, though; it just kind of was what it was, a mediocre piece of pizza. Nothing to think too hard about.

After finishing our slices, the four of us were sitting around digesting and talking bullshit when I absentmindedly dipped my finger into what seemed to be a puddle of grease. Let me be perfectly clear about my intentions here so you can fully understand what a disgusting slob I am: I was then going to lick the grease off my finger, and repeat that dip'n'lick process until the grease was gone. That's just me bein' me, okay? If you got a problem with it, you need to get some better problems, dog.

But listen: I didn't get to be a gross slob, because when I dipped my index finger into the grease, instead of grease wetting my fingertip (and whetting my appetite), it simply mushed down, semisolid, and retained an imprint of my finger. It was roughly the texture of congealing candle wax. I pointed at the plate in horror. Each member of our party gasped in turn, like witnesses at the scene of an accident.

One by one, Caroline, Greta, and Phoebe each dipped a finger into a puddle of grease on their plates and drew it back, aghast. "This is happening inside our bodies," I said very gravely. "We're all gonna die."

"Wait a minute," Phoebe chimed in. "It's the wax paper the slice came on!" And we all breathed a sigh of relief.

But Caroline was skeptical. "I don't know; I've had a lot of pizza on wax paper before, and I've never seen anything like this in my life."

I noticed a small bit of grease on my paper plate and, with

trepidation, reached my hand forward to touch it, hoping it was regular liquid grease. I mushed my finger into it and, sure enough, came away with a dry finger, leaving a dented pile on my plate. "It's not the wax paper," I reported.

I felt confident that we were in the beginnings of a situation like that in the classic horror film *The Stuff*. After having touched the substance on that plate, it seemed likely to me that an edible and delicious alien species was beginning its parasitic invasion of earth, abetted by greedy corporate bosses who were facilitating its spread because it created a ravenous consumer base. Soon the four of us, and countless others, would all be lining up outside Fat Sal's every day to get our fix. Eventually we'd turn into straight-up zombies, and shortly thereafter our heads would explode.

I was imagining (out loud) the brutal fate we were all about to suffer in incredible detail when Phoebe got up abruptly, muttering, "Enough talk. It's time for answers."

She walked over to the register, her back to us, chatting with the pizza man. We were all awed by her cool, calm demeanor, even more so when the pizza man smiled obligingly and invited her behind the counter. I thought I noticed something sinister in his smile and feared she was a goner, but a few moments later she strode back to the table, utterly satisfied with herself.

"It's lard," she told us triumphantly. "I went over to the counter and said to the guy, 'I just really liked the slice here; do you think I could take a look at where you guys make it?' And he took me back behind the counter, and there were just tubs and tubs of lard."

My famous friend Phoebe—Cool Mom and Cunning Detective. Who knew?

At this point you may be wondering whether eating so much pizza in one day compromised our ability to judge slices objectively, but I'd like to reassure you that it didn't. First of all, we didn't each get our own slice at every place. At most spots, Caroline and I split one slice while Phoebe and Greta split another. Second, as with all Harvesting Missions, it was just as much about enjoying one another's company as it was about eating pizza, so we took our time; we idled at tables to talk, we walked slowly between places. Eating at six or seven pizzerias took up the bulk of an afternoon, and when you factor in the slice-sharing, there was no risk of mouth fatigue or lapses in judgment.

Still, after Fat Sal's, each of us was maybe beginning to reconsider our love for pizza. But we continued, because we had to—and let me tell you, I'm so glad we did. The next place we went to, Gino's, on Eighty-Third Street between First and Second Avenues, served the best slice I had eaten in months. In years, maybe! The place was a dream come true. It was a little fancier looking than I was used to, but it wasn't off-putting.

There is a picture of my maternal grandfather and his brother standing on Astoria Boulevard in Queens sometime in the late twenties or early thirties that's been hanging in my parents' house for as long as I can remember. It's a great picture—for me, an iconic image of American Masculinity. When I moved out I made a print of it to hang in my new apartment. It's been with me in every place I've ever lived. My grandfather is standing on the right, taller and slimmer than his brother, wearing a nice-looking overcoat, a nice hat, and some well-worn but shined shoes. He looks to be in his mid-twenties. He's handsome, if gaunt. He looks serious. His right hand is in his coat pocket; his left is casually holding a cigarette. To his right is his brother, shorter and broader, with thick, dark eyebrows and an equally stern expression. He's coatless, wearing a double-breasted pin-striped suit and his own nice hat and well-worn shoes. He's got a cigarette in his mouth, and his hands are poised to strike a match.

In that picture my grandfather looks like a movie star; his brother looks like a mob boss or a boxer. They exude a certain rough sophistication and look nothing like the old men I barely remember, stooped from years of manual labor, who died during my early childhood. Neither of the men in the picture had a high school education; both of them would spend the rest of their lives working with their hands. They weren't the rich, influential men I perceive them to be when I look at the picture; they were a couple of working class jerks from Queens. In that photo, they portray a timeless sense of style, a personal aesthetic that defies class status.

Gino's looks like that picture. It's definitely a little ritzier than Pizza Palace, for instance, but it doesn't put on airs. It doesn't purport to be better than me. Which is sort of what Phoebe is like, come to think of it. I mean, in one sense, she lives in this mythic world that countless adults and children daydream about being part of. She's a movie star. And her husband is also a movie star. They probably hang out with other movie-star couples and do movie-star things together. But sitting around in a pizza place with her, you wouldn't know it.

Really, though, none of this old-world charm would matter for a fucking second if Gino's didn't make fantastic pizza. This slice was damn near perfect—excellent ratios, delicious ingredients, skillfully cooked to a slight char but without burning the mouth upon first bite. The cheese was plentiful but not overwhelming, and the sauce was delicately seasoned. Both were laid atop an exceptional foundation of bread that crunched *just right* with each bite.

Gino's was a milestone moment for Slice Harvester. I had eaten all the pizza Uptown and on the Upper West Side, and although a few places charmed me and a few slices impressed me, I hadn't been blown away until I took my first bite of the slice at Gino's. It felt like an affirmation, as if everything I was doing was worthwhile. If I were to run into Jamie on the street tomorrow, I could give him my awesome new zine and tell him about this great slice I'd found on the Upper East Side, of all fucking places.

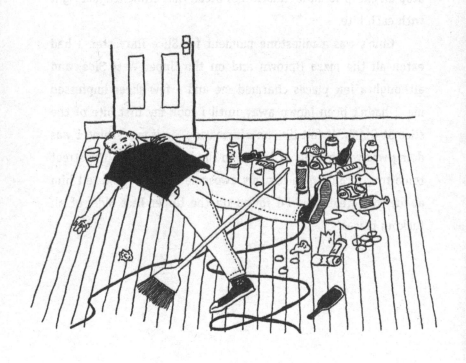

CHAPTER 4

La Crosta

Initially I was a little skeptical when I saw the phrase "Gourmet Pizzeria" on the awning of La Crosta Restaurant, but it was quickly clear that it was an empty platitude. There was a certain banality about this pizzeria, and a destitute resignation in its employees, that made me think of Samuel Beckett.

—*Slice Harvester Quarterly*, Issue 4, "Forty-Second to Fifty-Ninth Streets," visited on February 8, 2010

Opposite page: The morning after the show

At the beginning of February 2010 I had just turned twenty-seven and begun my Saturn Returns. This is astrology stuff, and I believe in it because I'm one of those New Age kooks, okay? Fuck you. Basically, Saturn is your father planet, and when you turn twenty-seven it shows up and is like, *What have you done with your life, you loser?* And if you're healthy and comfortable in your own skin (aka if you keep it really real), then things are good, but if you're in denial about stuff or not totally psyched about yourself (aka you're a poser), then times are rough and tough like leather and you're put through constant trials in order to overcome your character flaws and become a better person. Mostly you wanna just be like, *Whatever, Dad!* but actually you can't do that to Saturn because he will end you.

Saturn tricked me into thinking I had my shit together, because some totally awesome things happened in my first few weeks as a twenty-seven-year-old. The debut issue of *Slice Harvester Quarterly* came out, and I made enough money from zine sales to pay my rent that month. Admittedly, my rent was $450, but c'mon! Since I was thirteen I had dreamed of one day at least sort of supporting myself from punk stuff, but I never thought it would actually happen. I had a release party at the cool used bookstore that my friends had opened where I read really well and charmed everybody. In some ways, life was pretty grand.

That year seemed to be, at least in my circle, the moment right before it became socially acceptable to acknowledge that you trolled the web for dates. Today, everyone I know who isn't in a relationship has an online dating profile and talks about it. But back then it felt like a big, shameful secret. Usually I was safe in my solitude, awkwardly scouring the internet for love—punks are notoriously averse to adopting new forms of technology—but occasionally I would accidentally happen upon the profile of someone I knew socially.

One night I was at a show in a friend's living room, quite drunk, and realized that a woman at the show was someone whose dating profile I had seen. An important aspect of these sites is that they show you who has been looking at your profile, and people whose profiles you've seen are notified as well, so I knew she knew, and I knew she knew I knew she knew, too. At some point she cornered me in one of the bedrooms where a bunch of folks were hanging out doing drugs.

"So you're on OkCupid, too, huh?"

I shoved my hands into my pockets and looked at my feet while I spoke. "Yeah, uh, I guess. And you obviously are, too . . ." I trailed off.

"Yeah, duh. What are you, embarrassed about it? Who cares? It's not like I'm looking to fall in love on that thing. *That* would be embarrassing." She looked me dead in the face. "I mean, *you're* not looking to fall in love, right?"

"Yeah, no, of course not! Hah, love! Fuck that shit . . . Damn, is that Shit City Kids starting? I really wanted to see them. I'm gonna head into the living room."

And then I proceeded to never make eye contact with her again for at least a year.

Because I *was* hoping to meet someone to fall in love with, and I knew that the desire to fall in love with someone was pitiful, juvenile, NOT PUNK. Not that punk has a rulebook, though things would probably have been easier for me if we had something like Talmudic or Sharia law. Instead, punk's stringent rules are all unspoken, implied. Part of being jumped into the gang is slowly figuring out the rules and learning to adhere to them without ever putting voice to them or acknowledging their existence.

These rules change from year to year and scene to scene (in New York, for instance, or at least the New York of my youth, it was totally unacceptable to like sports—but go to Milwaukee and all the punks watch baseball. Hell, some of them even *play* baseball! Totally weird), but in the mid to late 2000s in the Brooklyn punk scene I was part of, monogamy and love were passé, outmoded leftovers from Victorian times. At least that's how it felt to me, because I am an idiot and see everything as strictly binary rather than as a nuanced gradation.

There were a lot of prominent voices in my community who wanted to love differently than the ways endorsed by our Sick Fucking Society. They said, "Monogamy is not the *only* thing in the world. There are other ways to be healthy and fulfilled, and we'd like the freedom to explore them without anyone's unsolicited and pernicious moralizing." Conceptually, this is totally sensible. However, listening to these conversations, all I really heard was "Monogamy is stupid and for squares, and if that's what you want to do, you are a stupid square yuppie poser and you were never punk and you never will be!"

So I tried really hard to live all freewheeling and fancy free, but the truth is, not only did I never feel comfortable with promiscuity, I was also bad at it. In order to succeed at practicing healthy nonmonogamy, you need good communication skills and a driving desire to share yourself with multiple partners. I possessed neither of those things. I began to approach romantic trysts with a sense of dread—as if they were an obligation, a chore. I was doing my duty to help forge a beautiful new world where everyone could pursue their true desires without fear of reprisal, but in doing so I had to shut down the voice inside myself telling me that the thing I actually wanted was a boring, stable, committed monogamous relationship, because that was just my bourgeois socialization talking, right? RIGHT?!

Then I met Christina.

Sometime in January, a few days after I went Slice Harvesting with Phoebe and Greta, my witch friend in Philly e-mailed me and told me I should fall in love with her best friend, Christina, who lived in New York. She told me we had very compatible astrological charts and sent me a picture of Christina sitting in front of a giant pizza, grinning. I thought she was absolutely beautiful, and I told the Good Witch of Philly as much over Gchat.

PizzaLuvr420: she's gorgeous! tell me more about her.
PhillyWitch69: she's an Aries, Virgo rising, moon in
Scorpio. she hates most men. she's perfect for you.

And then the Good Witch gave me Christina's e-mail, and I e-mailed her and she e-mailed me back. When she gave me her phone number she said, "Call me if you wanna talk. And if you're ever in a bad mood and need to take it out on someone, call this number and ask for Manoff," and she gave me another number with no real explanation. I never did call him. I assumed incorrectly that she must be a dominatrix and this dude was one of her johns, and part of their thing was that she had her potential suitors humiliate him over the phone. I've had a handful of friends who were sex workers, so I certainly didn't judge. Maybe I even thought it was cool.

When I later asked her for some clarification about who this Manoff guy was, she explained that she was a hostess at a hamburger restaurant in Union Square and that Manoff was a consistently rude dick and bad tipper to her delivery guys, so she wanted payback on their behalf and figured that if I called him and gave him shit, it wouldn't get traced back to her job, and the delivery guys wouldn't get in trouble. Basically, she was saying, "Colin, I am your dream girl."

We both wanted to hang out, and one night we agreed she would come over at 12:30 when she got out of burger work. That night I paced my apartment and chugged an entire six-pack of tall cans to calm my nerves before Christina arrived.

At this point, my drinking was completely out of hand. I had come off a three-month dry spell and was hitting the booze twice as hard to make up for lost time. I was no longer drinking during the day (at least, not *every* day), which was obviously a plus and led me to believe that I was "in control," but I would drink *so much* every night. This Dry Season–Rainy Season dichotomy had become cyclical in my life, like a weather pattern.

I had begun experimenting with sobriety a month after Jamie died. When he was still alive, the relentless drug use and partying among my circle of friends felt like a rejection of the Capitalist Death Cult and an acceptance of the impermanence of life. We lived in a fucked-up world that wasn't getting any bet-ter, and so we might as well squeeze every drop of life we could out of every second we got. Today is here, right now, and tomor-row is probably gonna suck, so let's get fucked-up.

It's like this: imagine Robocop laid a giant pizza in front of you and said, "If you eat this pizza, you'll be sick, but if you don't eat this pizza, you'll be sad." What would you do? In case it's unclear, in this analogy Robocop is global capitalism/"the man," you are me, and the pizza is partying. I had decided when I was pretty young that I'd rather be sick then sad.

After Jamie was gone, the partying didn't feel life-affirming anymore; it felt like a death trip, as if we were all lining up to be next. My own alcoholism was becoming more and more en-trenched in my life, and thus, ironically, more invisible to me. I knew my drinking was problematic, so I dealt with it by taking "time off," which solved a number of superficial problems. Any periods of sobriety or clean living I had were predicated on the promise of a return to my savage lifestyle. First off, I wasn't tak-ing breaks in order to maintain my physical health or sanity—I was taking breaks because I knew my relationship with booze was unsustainable, and I needed distance from that relationship in order to create sustainability: abstinence today for a drink to-morrow. Second, these occasional breaks created the illusion of agency in a situation that was no longer under my control. And so a pattern had emerged: get off booze for a week, a month, whatever; return to drinking with a newfound appreciation for clarity and moderation; then quickly fall back into drinking too much and blacking out every night because it was just so much easier than being alone with myself.

The point is, by the time I met Christina I was still getting ADAP (As Drunk As Possible) AAT (At All Times) in order to blot out any self-awareness that might interfere with me enjoying life or "experiencing the moment" or whatever. And that's what I did while I was freaking out with nervousness before she came over. I drank ninety-six ounces of Budweiser in a little under two hours and then slammed an entire pot of coffee to "get my head straight."

She rang my buzzer promptly at 12:30. When she came inside she was more beautiful than I ever could have imagined from the pictures I'd seen—shaved head, dark eyes, dressed like a total freak. We sat down at my table by the window to talk and smoke (she smoked!), and I offered up a mostly full bottle of chilled dessert wine I'd stolen from a catering company I worked for intermittently. I poured us each a glass, and we began to talk. I was still nervous and ended up drinking most of the wine.

Christina was twenty-three years old. She had been in the city for five years. She had gone to FIT to study fashion illustration but was stuck in the noncommittal food-service job cycle. She was beautiful and confident and seemed really cool. I stammered nervously about Slice Harvester, about traveling, being punk. I felt like an asshole.

Christina hadn't even come over until after midnight, so it was three or three thirty when our hangout felt like it was wrapping up. I didn't want her taking the bus home alone at such a late hour, so I invited her to stay over. I solemnly swear that I had nothing but the most noble intentions. Not to say that wanting to bone is ignoble, and not that I wasn't *interested* in the idea of some sort of eventual coupling; it just felt like it was too soon. Regardless, as we made our way into my room, I got really nervous that I was somehow gonna blow it because I was so drunk. She has since told me that she thought I was a complete weirdo whom she never wanted to see again, and had decided that she would just lie awake in bed until five thirty when the buses resumed regular, consistent service.

My mattress was on the floor of my tiny bedroom, underneath a loft bed my friend Paulie had recently been living on during a brief respite from his tramping through the Americas. The loft was now stacked with milk crates full of books, cassette tapes, old show fliers—sentimental detritus. My diminutive room was like a little rat's nest, stuffed with junk and trinkets I had dragged in from the street and which I would shove aside to clear space for sleeping. My one window looked out on the air shaft in the center of my ancient tenement building (constructed in 1865!), and the light from a full moon filtered in through the filthy, curtainless windows.

We sat on the edge of the mattress and talked for a while, about what I don't remember. At a certain point, when it felt right, I leaned in closer and asked, "Can I kiss you?"

Christina recoiled and stared straight at me, hands on her hips. "Who do you think I am? I just met you. *Jesus*. You ruined it."

I was so distraught I had to lie down. "I know I ruined it, but what did I ruin?" I asked, agonized.

She leveled a devastating gaze at me. "I don't know what you ruined, either, but I know you ruined it," she said, maybe with a hint of a smile, and she laid down on the bed with her back to me.

There we were, her at the very edge of the mattress, me on

my back next to the wall, staring up at the bottom of the loft and wondering how to fix things. We lay like that for what felt like an eternity but was probably only four or five minutes, after which we started talking again. Things returned to normal, or whatever approximates normal when lying in bed with someone you've known for only a few hours. She inched in from the edge of the bed and I came over from the wall, both of us moving incrementally, until our bodies were touching. As we talked I stroked her shaved head.

Eventually she turned around and kissed me, and it felt like the whole world melted. We kissed for a while. It felt like forever and like no time at all. But when we stopped kissing the moonlight had been replaced by the first rays of dawn, and when we looked out the window we realized it was snowing. We lay on our backs with our heads hanging upside down off the mattress and watched the snow fall up, holding hands. We dozed a bit, asleep in each other's arms, and I felt comfortable and whole. My feelings about her were very Modern Lovers right off the bat: *I Wanna Sleep In Your Arms*. But also, *I could bleed in sympathy with you / On those days*, despite the fact that we had just met. I am someone who has spent most of my life feeling out of place in the world and in my own body, but I felt at peace and at ease in Christina's embrace. When we finally woke up for good, Christina had to go home before work. I walked her to the door but not all the way down to the bus, because I am not a full gentleman and I was too hungover to put clothes on and walk down to the street.

We ended up hanging out again a few days later. Christina was sick, and I made her a giant pot of split pea soup with the ham bone that had been sitting in my freezer since Christmas. It was delicious soup. I served her a bowl with a circle-A drawn in hot sauce on the top, an old habit, and garnished with a few wayward cat hairs, like most meals in my house.

After we ate, I bundled her up and made her a cup of hot tea, and we got into bed together to watch movies, but ended up making out the whole time instead, despite the fact that she was sick. Right off the bat she and I were compatible on some deeply pheromonal level—being near Christina gave me a sense of peace I generally lacked, peace I had sought in other relationships and partners but had been unable to find.

It's almost embarrassing to describe the role that Slice Harvester played in this process. But for real—writing the blog and publishing the zines had massively improved my sense of self-worth. Looking back, it almost seems foolish. "Oh, yeah, so I did this thing where I reviewed all the pizza in Manhattan, and in conjunction with a really wonderful relationship, it taught me how to love myself." That sounds so cheesy, but it's true. It's also true that Christina played a huge role in my burgeoning adulthood, and yet I did everything I could to keep her at arm's length and make sure she couldn't help me at all, because my self-destructive behaviors were so deeply entrenched that they had developed their own defense mechanisms.

Despite all this inner turmoil bubbling so deep within me that it would take months to rise to the surface, Slice Harvesting was going well. A month before I met Christina, around the same time the Good Witch was beginning her elaborate matchmaking process, I went out pizza eating with my friend/colleague/cool older punk dude Erick Lyle, whose belief in the value of the project helped set me on the path to believing in myself. He had just put out *Scam* issue 5½, "The Epicenter of Crime: The Hunt's Donuts Story," which is possibly my favorite single issue of any zine ever. Erick is a supertalented writer and an encouraging older person, and he was quick to realize that my pizza project was cool even if I was a bit of a self-deprecator. Though he doesn't necessarily have the most nurturing personality, he tried to bolster my sense of self-worth in the kind manner of a childless adult trying to teach his friend's kid a lesson in self-esteem.

Erick also brought a lens through which to filter our pizza eating. After we finished our first slice at Italian Village on First Avenue on the Upper East Side, he pulled a copy of Frank O'Hara's *Lunch Poems* from his bag. "I figured he may have been in this neighborhood when he wrote these poems, so we can use them to describe the pizza." This was maybe the best idea I had ever heard.

So without further ado, here is a list of the pizza places I ate at with Erick on January 27, 2010, rated on a scale of *Lunch Poems*. Make of it what you will.

Italian Village, 1526 First Avenue:
where is the summit where all aims are clear
the pin-point light upon a fear of lust

Don Filippo, 1133 Lexington Avenue:
instant coffee with slightly sour cream
in it, and a phone call to the beyond

Pizzcafe Express, 1107 Lexington Avenue:

in the rancid nourishment of this mountainous island
they are coming and we holy ones must go

La Mia Pizza, 1488 First Avenue:

yet I do not explain what exactly
makes me so happy today

Ciao Bella Napoli, 1477 York Avenue:

and I'll be happy here and happy there, full
of tea and tears. I don't suppose I'll ever get
to Italy, but I have the terrible tundra at least.

Figaro Pizza, 1469 Second Avenue:

when the tears of a whole generation are assembled
they will only fill a coffee cup

Erick didn't know this, but a huge part of why I got into
punk and made zines and played music was an attempt to as-
sert myself into a continuum of Cool Weirdos that I believe has
existed throughout history. Tuli Kupferberg, Sylvia Rivera, Sun
Ra, Hannah Höch—these are the Old Gods I light candles for and
leave offerings to (weed for Tuli, pills for Sylvia, tea for Sun Ra,
coffee for Hannah). I don't know much about Frank O'Hara, but
I bet he's a plain slice kinda guy.

CHAPTER 5

Pizza Villagio

If we aren't careful, pizza will be stripped of all of its nuance and merit and sucked into the Capitalist Death Culture. . . . But as long as there are still a few old, surly pizza men scowling at their customers and serving up warm, greasy slices, we still have a chance in this war!

—*Slice Harvester Quarterly*, Issue 4, "Forty-Second to Fifty-Ninth Streets," visited March 11, 2010

One hundred forty-six slices in, I met up with my friend Aaron Cometbus to eat pizza in Midtown. In terms of chosen family, Aaron is like my uncle or cool older cousin—in other words, he's my still-fallible older male role model. This dynamic is aided by the fact that he is, like, one hundred feet tall and has long limbs and gigantic hands—a true Jewish sentinel—and an oftentimes stern face. He's handsome, for sure—good cheekbones, great head of hair—but he can look very serious. (I suspect that once upon a time as a teenager in Berkeley he was doing his Billy Idol impression when the wind changed and his face got stuck like that.) His sheer size combined with the gravity of his expression make it easy to feel like a nephew standing next to him.

A. C. has been involved with punk forever. He started writing songs and playing in bands before I was even born. I read his zines and listened to his records in high school and imagined what it would be like when I was grown up and would actually be able to relate to his stories on an experiential rather than imaginary level. It never crossed my mind that one day we would be friends. I'd like to take a minute to appreciate that, because I realize I'm very lucky. Not lucky to be friends with Aaron in particular—I feel lucky to have all my friends. No, I'm talking about the phenomenon of having someone whose work

I've admired and who I looked up to for years now calling me sometimes just to see how I'm doing. Even though I don't think about it often, because our friendship would be weird if I did, I know that not everyone is afforded the opportunity to befriend their teenage heroes.

(And I also know that all the punks are super over it and probably take a lot of the awesome aspects of our community for granted, but I am also lucky enough to have this weird pizza-worshipping audience [that includes you, dear reader] of folks who haven't been punk their whole lives, and that's who I'm talking to right now. So, FYI, one of the things that's great about our little community is that there aren't really "celebrities" as such, and those who pass for the closest approximation thereof are still just people you see around who hang out and go to shows.)

Anyway, a while ago I sent a stack of fanzines to Sam McPheeters, the former singer of Born Against, a relatively popular local hardcore band that has gained increasing notoriety since its dissolution over twenty years ago. McPheeters had recently published an incredible novel that I read and enjoyed immensely, so I wrote him to tell him as much. Less than a week later, I got a postcard back, thanking me for my kind words and letting me know how excited he was to read my zines. Contrast that with other folks I've reached out to who aren't punks: when I was sixteen, I sent Katherine Dunne, author of *Geek Love*, a very similar package. I still haven't heard back from her. Maybe two years ago I sent a big stack of zines to Ed Sanders from the Fugs, who I see, in many ways, as a sort of creative grandfather figure. I wrote him what I thought was an incredibly charming letter, which read:

Dear Ed Sanders,

I am writing to see if you'd like to be friends. It won't
require much! Mostly I'd just like your permission to
say "my friend Ed Sanders from the Fugs" rather than
just saying "Ed Sanders from the Fugs" when I refer to
you, which I do frequently, as I immensely admire your
work as a musician, writer, and publisher. Enclosed are
a few issues of my zine, which may not even exist if it
weren't for the work you did in paving the way for small
publishers with Fuck You Magazine *so many years ago.*
Thank you for that, and for so much more.

Yours,
Colin Atrophy Hagendorf

I included an addressed, stamped postcard to make writing back easier. Over a year later he sent it back, with one of his cool, weird triptychs hand-drawn onto it, but no text. I, of course, took this as a tacit endorsement of my request, and have referred to him as "my friend Ed Sanders" ever since (though I was a little disappointed that my package wasn't the beginning of an epic intergenerational postal correspondence).

The few people who saw the postcard from Ed Sanders when it came in the mail thought it was so cool he had written to me at all that I felt ungrateful feeling let down. It was only when I sat in that first pizzeria with A. C. that I was finally reassured that my feelings weren't totally fucked-up.

"I finally heard back from Ed Sanders," I told Aaron. He

perked up. He's also a huge Fugs fan, so I had told him ages ago when I sent off the original package. "Yeah, it didn't say anything, but he drew one of those sigils that he draws on it."

Aaron grimaced and shook his head slightly. "You can't win 'em all."

Don't get me wrong—it's so rad that Ed Sanders sent me a postcard. He's getting older and he's busy, and he probably doesn't have time to make friends with all of his fans. Although maybe there was something more to decipher in his triptych, and if I had been fluent in ancient hippie ideographs, I could have decoded a long and amicable letter. Who knows?

(Ed: If you're reading this, the offer is still on the table. If you would like to be my friend, I would be honored.)

But back to Aaron, who, despite his best intentions, is the authorial voice of the closest thing we have to a Hammurabi's Code in the punk community. For myself and many others who read them as teenagers, his tour diaries and fiction about punk houses laid out a framework for what our adult punk lives might look like. His zines have functioned throughout the years as an almost ethnographic study of various facets of punk. His "Back to the Land" issue, in which he interviewed the children of parents who went "back to the land" in the 1960s, as well as those of his peers who did the same of their own volition, is a straightforward sociological study. In many ways, his zines read as a litany of his friends' failures and shortcomings, a list of disappointments. I know that's not something he did intentionally; it takes a pretty self-conscious and uncomfortable reader such as myself to interpret Aaron's stories of fumbling young adulthood so pessimistically, but that's how they felt to me: a list of the ways in which life could go wrong, peppered with a few transcendent moments where everything seems to work out.

Did you ever read *A Canticle for Leibowitz* by Walter M. Miller, Jr.? If not, you should. It's awesome. It takes place far in the future. As the story goes, sometime around Right Now, there was a big nuclear holocaust. Subsequently, a bunch of survivors got together and started killing all the remaining scientists and destroying their books in order to return to a simpler, more agrarian society and avoid further calamity at the hands of Science Run Amok. (Kind of like Pol Pot, but kind of not at all like Pol Pot.) So this dude Isaac Leibowitz, a Jewish engineer, started saving books and hiding them away. He converted to Catholicism and founded an order of monks dedicated to preserving books and history, but eventually he got killed and a lot of the books got wrecked. The novel predominantly takes place hundreds of years after all this happened, and it's about the remaining monks in the Order of Leibowitz trying to piece together history from their scant supply of the previous culture's books. Like I said, it's really cool.

Now pretend that instead of a physical landscape destroyed by nuclear fallout, there are the suburbs, a cultural landscape rendered barren by capitalism. And instead of there being *no* books, there are *a bunch* of books—my mom and dad's Sartre texts and Dostoevsky novels, as well as newspapers and magazines and textbooks. And instead of an order of monks, there is only me. But then have me reading issues of *Cometbus* like those monks in the Order of Leibowitz were reading the Only Books Left. That's basically what it was like when I was a teenager and early twentysomething.

I had this conception of Aaron that was borderline mythic. I mapped together this piecemeal time line of cities that he had lived in, based on stories in his zines and the content of some of his band's songs, and I had this impression that he was solely responsible for there being thriving punk scenes in all these places. Like, "Oh, well, Aaron lived in Asheville and Chattanooga and Pensacola, and those places are all awesome and have really tight-knit punk communities today, so obviously the only logical thing is that he is some sort of kindly punk Johnny Appleseed who travels around the country turning disparate crews of reject teenagers into totally cohesive and awesome communities of artists." I've always had an overactive imagination. Still do.

The point I'm trying to make is that to me and a few other people in our small, parochial subculture, Aaron is something of a celebrity. And unlike most people who meet celebrities and are totally disenchanted to learn that their favorite singer/actor/athlete is not nearly as cool as he/she appears on the stage/screen/field, I have met Aaron Cometbus and eaten pizza with him, and he's obviously not as cool as I imagined he would be when I was fifteen, but he's way cooler than I thought he was when I was twenty—he is merely a man, after all.

Human though he is, the day I ate pizza with Aaron was one of the first moments when I really felt like I had arrived, like this thing I was doing *mattered*. The sense of personal accomplishment I felt at seeing my project embraced by someone whose work I had admired for years was far greater than that generated by being the subject of a fluff piece in the *Daily News* or watching the hit counter on my website rise exponentially. To use a nonfamilial metaphor, Aaron might be Jay Z, the older, wiser artist who defined the genre and who takes under his wing a young upstart. Though that would make me Kanye West; an unpleasant outcome, but so be it.

The day Aaron and I met up to go Harvesting was beautiful, and I rode my bike into the city for the first time in ages. When I was younger I worked as a messenger for a minute, and since then I've done a lot of delivery work, of food and, uh . . . other stuff. Being forced to ride my bike every day for work had taken some of the childlike glee out of it, but on this particular day it felt great—I was perfectly in tune with traffic, and all the lights seemed to be timed in my favor—an auspicious start.

I had gotten enough sleep and hadn't drunk *that* many beers the night before, so I wasn't hungover, even. I was alert and aware and running the streets. Riding a bike in New York City can be one of those mystical experiences in which you suddenly find yourself inexplicably in tune with the universe—like losing yourself in the music of an amazing band, kissing your sweetheart, or eating the perfect slice. By the time I got to the corner where Aaron was waiting I was exuberant, just bursting with energy. I hadn't even had coffee yet, but I was talking a mile a minute as we sat on the curb and smoked. It was disconcerting for Aaron, whom I had dragged out of bed a little earlier than he was accustomed to because I had to finish our pizza mission in time for some plans that night. The timing set us dead in the middle of the lunch rush, when slices are freshest. When a pizza parlor gets really busy, the slices don't get to sit for very long; they come out of the oven hot and get put right onto the waiting plates of hungry customers. I happen to think it's easiest to cook a slice well when it's cooked twice, so a place that can serve a perfect slice without reheating it is really something else.

We would be eating pizza at the top of Midtown—a bland place, somehow worse than the rest of Midtown. To the south, Times Square is a spectacle of consumer capitalism gone off the rails. To the west, Hell's Kitchen still has some lingering eccentricities from when it was the immigrant slum in which *West Side Story* took place. To the east is Turtle Bay, dark and ominous, full of diplomatic missions; it looks like the streets in the film *Dark City*, a classic New York noir. But the area in between it all? There's nothing there. Tall gray buildings, too generic to feel intimidating; they could be the fabricated backdrop in a movie or in some urban adventure video game.

The pizzerias were mostly boring shitholes that Aaron compared to the cafeterias that populate Isaac Bashevis Singer's New York, a comparison I readily agreed to, though I had no idea what he was talking about, having only read Singer's shtetl stories. A few months later I bought a copy of *A Friend of Kafka* at Aaron's bookstore, and sure enough, many of the stories pan out in bland Midtown eateries.

None of the pizza we ate that day was any good, but there was one place that was at least interesting: Buk Balkan Bistro on West Fifty-Fifth Street. The outside of Buk looked recently remodeled, and the inside seemed like it could be any other bar/ restaurant in any other whatever neighborhood in Manhattan.

"I guess this place isn't a pizzeria anymore," I told Aaron.

"Might as well start heading to the next place. It's like that sometimes; I get a phone book listing for a pizza place, but by the time I get there it's a new business."

Aaron was unconvinced and peered in the window. "I don't know, Colin," he said. "I think I see a pizza oven in there." He headed in the door.

Buk turned out to be a fully staffed fancy restaurant—which was jarring after our afternoon spent munching cheese pies in crummy cafeterias. There was a bartender wearing a little waistcoat, a waiter standing at attention, and an older, demure maître d', who perked up at his host stand as the door opened. He looked us up and down, taking in our filthy shoes, dirty fingernails, and greasy hair, and just barely avoided having an expression of visible disappointment cross his face before turning on his charm.

"Table for two?"

"Do you serve pizza here?" I asked hesitantly, looking around.

"Of course, pizza, right this way," he said as he led us to a marble counter with a pizza oven behind it.

"We're just going to split one slice, if that's okay." (At this point I would not have blamed him for rolling his eyes, but he remained a perfect gentleman.)

"Absolutely, whatever you like, sir; have a seat." He pointed us toward a high bar table flanked by two stools. There was a tea light in a small glass votive, a single flower, and those tiny salt and pepper shakers, all arranged artfully atop a white table-cloth. A *tablecloth*.

A few minutes passed, and he brought us our slice, which

was not disgusting but not great, and was *definitely* not the same kind of pizza I was accustomed to eating. Perhaps this was Balkan pizza? Or maybe some Albanian dude here in New York wrote his cousin in Kosovo and said, "Here in America we have this thing called pizza!" and described the pizza. And then the cousin told her best friend, and the best friend told her uncle, and the uncle told his apprentice, and the apprentice eventually moved to New York and started a pizza place based on this telephone game of what pizza was like before even trying a real New York slice. It was enough like pizza to seem normal at first, but went slightly awry in difficult-to-pinpoint, subtle ways—it was slightly off-color, the texture was alien, the sauce was flavored by spices that I'd never before encountered. The whole experience of eating this slice was disconcerting. This was the Uncanny Valley of pizza. It was also the greasiest slice I have ever eaten in my life, which is an incredible accomplishment.

When we got outside, I asked Aaron why he'd been so sure they would be serving pizza in a Balkan bistro.

"I don't know if you know this, Colin," he said with an air of gravitas, "but a lot of pizzerias are actually owned by Albanians who came to New York during the Kosovo War in the nineties."

(This was something I did actually know, mostly because Aaron had told me every time we'd talked about pizza for the past year. "It's an interesting story," he'd say with a wink and a nod. "There's a book in there somewhere.")

Every time I visit Aaron at the bookstore or when he's selling on the street, he's reading a different dusty, inscrutable tome about some obscure Eastern European war or African conflict. At first I thought it was an affectation. But Aaron seems to have a genuine interest in the forgotten factionalism of sectarian states or tribal conflicts the rest of the West has long closed the book on. I think it partially has to do with the fact that all of his identities are defined in strident opposition to those around him—punks, Jews, Berkeley natives. It is a characteristic of his that I appreciate immensely, especially when it results in my learning about the Albanian infiltration of the pizza industry.

At this point in my Harvesting career I'd eaten at nearly one hundred fifty pizza parlors, with over two hundred left to go. And I hadn't looked back once. Since that first day's Harvest with Sweet Tooth, I had been an eating/reviewing machine, filled with new purpose (and an abundance of dairy). Looking back on this ultraproductive period, I'm reminded of being thirteen years old, about to publish my first fanzine.

I had run off three hundred copies at the office supply store. The zine itself was garbage, most of the content cribbed from elsewhere—advertisements I had solicited from tiny bedroom record labels or straight-up cut out of *MRR* and pasted in; an e-mail forward of "The Fifty Best Pickup Lines" from the burgeoning days of AOL that a friend's older sister had sent me. With three hundred copies hot off the presses, I then stood outside the supermarket and tried to sell them to everyone going in or out. For comparison, most of my friends who made zines at the time printed five or ten total and never showed them to anyone.

It wasn't hubris or bravado that led me to make so many. I made zines in order to forge a connection between myself and the world around me, and it seemed that getting them to the most people possible was the best way to make that connection. Slice Harvester was the same, on an even grander scale—it was my letter to all of New York and the universe, beating out the Morse code that said, "I'm here. Where are you?"

And people responded! My friends, the older generation of punks, were proud of me, and that was great. But because I made the blog as well as the zine, because I stepped out of conventional punk channels, I connected with people who *weren't even punks!* This dude Ron started writing regular comments on my site. He's some dad from Long Island; we have nothing in common and never would have had any reason to interact, but over the course of his years of commenting, he's dropped little facts about his life. And now he's in this book. Hi, Ron!

At a certain point my weekly expenses of about $25 for pizza and train fare started to cut into my tight, young budget, so I placed a PayPal donation button on my webpage. I wrote a blog post mentioning that if people enjoyed the site, they should consider donating $2.50 (the average cost of a slice at the time) per month. The only reward I offered was that donators would be thanked publicly on the website and acknowledged in each issue of the fanzine. I wasn't looking to make a profit, and I don't think I ever really did, but over the two years that the blog ran, as long as I was regularly updating, I received these tiny donations from strangers to help me pay for the pizza. That's really something.

Listen to this one: I got a one-hundred-dollar discount on

a mattress because the guy at Sleepy's recognized me from the paper. He called me the "Slice Hunter," but who cares? That shit is crazy! All I had ever wanted as a kid was to create something that would resonate with people—and here I was, doing just that. It sure felt good.

My interactions with readers weren't all positive, but even the negative ones were lighthearted and ended up with everyone laughing and joking around. When I reviewed Artichoke, a trendy nouveau pizza place that had gotten famous for their simple menu, lack of seating, and boho décor, I took a pretty snotty tone, because I'm punk and an antagonist and that's what we do. My review opened:

> Every time I tell a *Time Out NY*-reading, condo-dwelling truffle eater about Slice Harvester, they ask me what I think about Artichoke, because they read about it in the *Times* or on some food blog and heard it was the best new shit. And every time they asked me I had to tell them, "I dunno." Because I hadn't gotten there yet. And now I have, and I had their "margherita" slice or whatever, which is not the artichoke slice, which I hear is *just to die faw*, but fuck it, whatever, who cares?

And this resulted in some dude accusing me of "reverse-snobbery," which resulted in me telling him that for the people wielding the power in 90 percent of situations, affluent yuppies sure do seem to get really defensive about being teased. Perhaps that's because they know their stranglehold on hegemonic influence is actually unfair, and maybe since, like, all of culture was presumably canted toward making people like this feel comfortable, they should learn to take a joke. Later that day, I received an anonymous $100 donation to my PayPal account, the donator choosing to be identified by the moniker "Yuppie Scum." I can't say for certain that Yuppie Scum and my anonymous commenter were the same guy, but it seems likely.

And there were other, more personal connections: getting a letter from Tobi Vail—OG riot grrrl, longtime zine maker, someone I'd admired since my adolescence—telling me she liked my fanzine; having Tom Scharpling, the greatest radio personality in American history, tweet that he liked my work; becoming friends with Ashok Kondabolu and Himanshu Suri from Das Racist because of a mutual creative admiration.

But it wasn't all victories. Slice Harvesting, and my life in general, were about to take a serious downturn before they could rise again like a pizza phoenix from the ashes of a burnt pie.

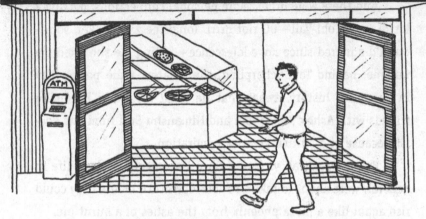

CHAPTER 6

Michelle's Restaurant

This may be the first good slice I've had in weeks. In the pizza desert that is Midtown West, Michelle's is a hidden oasis. This slice had wonderful, perfectly salty and crunchy dough. The sauce had that intangibly magical flavor that contributes to a slice without being overbearing, and the cheese had the perfect texture. You'd never think from passing by here that there was anything special lurking inside, but that's why I'm pounding the pavement, doing the hard work for you.

—*Slice Harvester Quarterly*, Issue 4, "Forty-Second to Fifty-Ninth Streets," visited on April 7, 2010

Opposite page: The Pronto Pizzas

I had walked nearly every block of Manhattan from 207th Street down to 50th, and had eaten more than 150 different slices of pizza. Almost a year had passed; I wasn't even halfway done, and the crappiness of most of the pizza was starting to weigh on me pretty hard. It seemed that for every Pizza Palace or Gino's there were fifteen shitty bodegas serving frozen slices out of a convection oven and calling themselves pizza places. I was almost done with the second issue of the fanzine, the Upper West Side issue, and aside from other people's art contributions, I wasn't too excited about it. Just a boring guy making a boring fanzine about boring pizza in a boring neighborhood.

The slice slump extended into my personal life. I was working this dumb burrito delivery job that didn't pay the bills, I was hungover all the time, the honeymoon period of my Saturn Returns was through, and though I put on a smile at the bar every night and pretended I was excited to be alive, the truth of the matter was that I was bored and listless and felt like crap every day. The only positive aspects of my life were my fanzine (selling enough to make rent!) and my relationship with Christina, which felt awesome even if I was on the verge of fucking it all up.

At twenty-seven, I was drinking to the point of blacking

out almost every night that I wasn't hanging out with Christina. And starting about halfway through April, every night at some point between five and seven in the morning, as I was lying in my bed chain-smoking (or in the bathroom of a bar where I'd stayed well past closing time), I'd call Christina and leave her long, rambling messages declaring my love for her, sometimes reciting Dylan Thomas poems into her voice mail and crying at their beauty. What a lucky gal, having a boyfriend who is totally cool and emotionless, and then gets drunk every night and becomes an inarticulate ball of unsorted emotional laundry.

You get the point. "I was fucked! In a rut! Something's gotta *giiiiiive!*" to quote a nonexistent Black Flag* song I just made up. The pizza in Midtown seemed to be mirroring where I was in life. Most of it was passable, some of it was terrible, and none of it was good. I didn't know what I should do—I just knew I had to keep eating. It was time to call in reinforcements.

I've known Cory since he moved out of his parents' house in Queens into a tent in the backyard of a notorious Brooklyn punk house as a teenager. He seems to have tapped into some kind of eternal spring of coolness that has probably existed as long as there has been human culture. Think Jim Jarmusch or MC Skat Kat from Paula Abdul's "Opposites Attract" video. Effortless cool. It's a different kind of cool than James Dean or young Snoop Dogg, because it's not dark. There's no lingering scent of death hovering around it. But Cory wasn't always cool. I watched him grow into it.

It's like this: growing up, I thought cats were these naturally

---

Jealous Again lineup.

graceful creatures who possessed some kind of ultimate insight and wisdom, an impression I had thanks mostly to my staring at them while super stoned or on mushrooms as a teenager. When I was twenty I got myself two kittens, Sal and Growler, and I remember having this realization one day (quite likely also while on mushrooms) as I watched baby Sal flop around awkwardly, trying unsuccessfully to jump up onto my dresser, that cats actually have to learn all that grace they seemed to possess innately, and that as kids they are not yet accustomed to their future graceful bodies. When I first met Cory, he was an awkward kitten, but now he is definitely a wise old cat. (This, by the way, is a totally inappropriate metaphor, as Cory is allergic to cats.) He is also the only person I know who doesn't look dumb wearing a fringed leather vest.

Nate Stark is also really cool, but in a more obscure way. I don't know if his last name is actually "Stark" or if that's just a descriptive punk name about his personality. Nate has a shaved head and a leather jacket, and he looks really serious all the time. Sometimes we stand on a street corner by the record store he works at in Williamsburg, just smoking and judging people. I know it's horrible, but it's cathartic, and frankly, the people of Williamsburg deserve to be judged.

He has also always played in only the coolest bands. I met him when he came to Brooklyn from out west to join Bent Outta Shape, Jamie's old band, and transform them from a band with the potential to be awesome into a band that totally ruled and made the world feel like a better place. Nate has been partially responsible for transporting me away from my constantly nagging anxieties and helping me to lose myself in the present, for recording one of my favorite records ever in the history of the universe, and for so much more. Actually, I don't really think there's any more, but those two are pretty good. I don't know whether I've ever thanked him for all this, because it would be awkward to do that in person. So here it is, awkwardly on paper: Thank you, Nate.

But the key quality in Nate-as-Harvesting-buddy was that he grew up in Berkeley and used to work in a pizza parlor there, which meant he could contribute meaningful insider knowledge to my ridiculous blog.

The three of us met up at the juncture of Forty-Seventh Street and Park Avenue, a relatively mundane corner in a relatively mundane part of Manhattan, featuring an even mix of cool-looking older buildings and totally ugly glass edifices. (I've been inside a lot of these buildings both as a bike messenger and while cooking for a catering company. At first it was exciting going into all the offices because it was, like, access to this weird world I would otherwise never be part of, but it turns out there's nothing interesting going on, and office buildings are just as boring as they seem.)

When most people think "Park Avenue," they think "elegant Old-Money rich people," and that is totally true of Park Avenue on the Upper East Side. Up there, the architecture is beautiful and imposing. It's like Mount Olympus, a place us mortals can visit but daren't stay. Every building is guarded by a stately door-man wearing a smart little suit, and you can tell that high above, behind the glare of those windows, all kinds of people with more money than you can possibly dream of are doing crazy BDSM shit to each other and neglecting their kids.

Down in Midtown, Park Avenue is a fairly mundane urban business district spruced up a bit by some giant planters filled with festive perennials on the pedestrian islands separating the lanes of north- and southbound traffic, as well as these pathetic paved promenades where office folk can sit, weather permitting, and enjoy their lunches. Many of the benches are marked with tiny brass placards stamped NO LOITERING, which seems contradictory for a bench, but if you put on your *They Live* glasses, you'll see that they actually say YOU CAN'T SIT HERE IF YOU'RE HOMELESS.

On the day we three jerkoffs showed up in Midtown, abutting one of these sad "parks" was a food truck. Not such a bizarre sight, as the Midtown lunch crowd absolutely *adores* buying food from trucks, but this particular truck purported to sell pizza, and that is weird, because there is enough pizza in New York already.

Historically, only a small number of foods have been proffered from carts in New York City—roasted nuts, hot dogs/knishes/pretzels, and Middle Eastern/halal fare; that's pretty much it, save for the awesome samosa cart that's been in Washington Square Park since before Christopher Columbus was born. Lately, however, food trucks have become "a thing," and now there are a million of them. They have cutesy names and Twitter accounts you can follow to find out where they're parked today, and guess what—I hate it all.

The thing about this pizza truck was that what they served bore only the slightest resemblance to pizza. We ordered a slice, and what they handed us was, like, some weird cracker with a bunch of soupy sauce on top. There turned out to be cheese beneath the sauce, but really, the whole mess should've been served in a bowl and eaten with a spoon. Now, the classic New York slice, when done right, is a perfect food to eat while standing or walking—it's self-contained and doesn't make a mess. So selling pizza from a truck kind of makes sense. But the decision to take a food that's easy to eat while standing and make it sloppier and more unwieldy and then sell it out of a truck to people walking by on the street is absolutely baffling, and it turned out to be a harbinger of things to come.

After that strange culinary experience, we made our way to an unpleasant-looking cafeteria on Forty-Eighth Street called Toasties. Long and fluorescent-lit, Toasties presented us with a number of nonpizza meal choices: a pathetic salad bar, steam trays full of dried-out pasta, plastic soda cups full of cotton-candy-pink yogurt. Tucked away in the very back was a pizza counter, which seemed inoffensive at best, but definitely not promising. But we were Men at Work, so we sucked it up, ordered a slice, and found a seat at one of the handful of empty tables. Aside from a couple of employees eating grim shift meals, we were the only folks who got our food to stay. It seems the clientele of Toasties—mostly solitary, white males dressed in business-casual wear—prefer to consume their sad paninis and salads elsewhere.

The pizza itself, while not horrendous, was *not* good. The dough was permissible. It didn't taste especially good or bad; it crunched, but not enough. In the end it neither added nor subtracted from the slice. The sauce, too, lacked any sort of presence, perhaps due to its sparse quantity. But what the slice lacked in sauce it made up for in cheese, which was plentiful, albeit disgusting. It's not that the cheese didn't have a taste so much as it had an antitaste. It tasted of *lack* of *absence.*

It bears noting that at one point this slice tried to kill Cory. He took what should have been an innocuous bite of an otherwise innocuous slice, and, seemingly of its own accord, the cheese expanded, filling his mouth and clogging his throat. He's a robust young man, so he was able to Heimlich himself back into well-being. If Toasties were an entity, I might think it was deliberately trying to harm us before we got outside and let everyone know how crappy their pizza is. Well, too bad, Toasties, we lived!

Invigorated from having cheated death, we continued west on Forty-Eighth to a magical subterranean establishment called Pronto Pizza & Beer (PP&B). Upon entering PP&B, we descended down a long sloping ramp until we were below street level. "This Is How We Do It" was playing on the radio, and it smelled faintly like a homeless guy or a traveling punk, which is a smell I associate with dear friends and is comforting to me. There were mirror-lined walls trimmed with red-and-white-striped molding, which met a green lower half—a not-so-subtle nod to the Italian flag. Cory called it "1991, the pizzeria," which seems apt, although I'm pretty sure he was born in 1987, so any knowledge he has of the early nineties is purely academic. I'll put it like this: I wouldn't have been surprised to see a NARC arcade game hanging out with an Addams Family pinball machine along one of the walls.

The swarthy, hirsute pizza man interrupted a phone conversation he was having in the thickest New York–accented Spanish I have ever heard to level a harsh gaze at me, his eyes flitting briefly toward Nate and Cory, who were lurking a few feet behind me like goons.

"One slice," I told him as confidently as possible.

He paused to adjust his backward Yankee hat and gestured to my crew with his impressive eyebrows. I could tell by the look on his face he knew what was coming. "What about them?" he asked.

"We're sharing," I responded, moderately scared that he'd kick us out and I wouldn't get to keep listening to Montell Jordan.

He wordlessly turned away, disgusted, and picked up a slice on his spatula and thrust it into the heat of the oven with palpable malice.

By the time he pulled it out, Cory and Nate had secured us a table, not that it was hard to do so. The place was cavernous. The clientele at PP&B were markedly younger and more diverse, in terms of both race and gender, than Toasties's. Where the latter seemed to draw in mostly solitary white businessmen, Pronto was populated by teen couples skipping school, guys wearing dusty coveralls, women talking briskly on Bluetooth headsets while nibbling on slices, and a small coalition of Haggard Ancients.

A funny thing, though: the atmosphere may have been better than that at Toasties, but the pizza wasn't. It felt careless. The dough was too thick and tasted like oven cleaner. The sauce had no flavor, yet managed to add an unpleasant moistness to the slice. The cheese was too salty. Texturally, Nate described it as similar to "accidentally chewing on plastic." The crust was an afterthought that practically fell off when I folded the slice, as if extra dough had been hastily added on after the pie's initial foundation had already been laid.

It's a real shame, because a place that looks this good is hard to come by. It takes years of airborne grease and neglected hygienic practices to create an ambience that is so perfectly attuned to all of my aesthetic sensibilities. And the things that were wrong with this pizza were basically products of negligence. In other words, this pizza might not have been such a dick if it had any self-esteem.

This slice was, like, the Anthony Kiedis of pizza. I've been reading that guy's memoir, and it's clear that he is not the best guy. Genuinely selfish and narcissistic, he doesn't seem to have the capacity to empathize with women and talks about sleeping with teenagers well into his twenties in this blasé manner that I find totally disgusting. I could list his other negative qualities at length; they're readily apparent. The other thing that is very apparent from his memoir, though, is that his childhood was clearly really fucked-up. But, like, even though that's sad, and even though it's possible Kiedo might be a better person if his life had been a little less sordid. I still think he's a turd of a man. Do you see what I'm getting at about the pizza? Just because this slice might've been better if someone cared about it a little more doesn't mean we didn't have a fucking miserable experience eating it.

I still had a long list of pizza parlors for us to hit that day, so we did our best to remain undaunted. It wasn't easy. This was my moment of doubt. The seemingly rapid pace at which I had been going was beginning to dwindle, and I was losing focus. I was beginning to wonder if I even wanted to finish. I mean, what was the point, right? And what was I doing with my life, anyway? I lived in a shitty, crumbling old tenement in the neighborhood my father had grown up in and busted his ass to get out of. I drank till I blacked out every night, and didn't really see any reason to stop. I needed some kind of inspiration, some reminder of why I had started in the first place, but the pizza I'd eaten so far on this particular day didn't make me feel like any galvanizing moments were forthcoming.

Of course, I didn't have time to think too hard about my disappointing life or disappointing pizza, because our next stop was actually on the same block as Pronto Pizza & Beer. And get this—it was called Pronto Pizza as well! Perhaps they were related? Maybe they were rivals? Maybe they were once related, owned by brothers or cousins, but had become rivals after a familial spat? I couldn't wait to find out, as I do love a good blood feud.

Walking past the sixteen storefronts between the two Pronto Pizzas was like entering a weird science fiction future where nationalities were a thing of the past, their only remnants a bunch of ethnic fast-food chains. At the time of this Harvest, there was a Maki Sushi, Hing Won Express Noodle Shop, Indus Express, and a Pig 'n' Whistle Irish Pub on that street, plus a dental office, a loan place, an off-track betting establishment, and a psychic. It was all of New York City in five hundred filthy feet. And just for good measure, a giant parking garage took up the entire north side of the block.

Cory, Nate, and I soon learned that Pronto Pizza (henceforth referred to as PP) was like a bizarre, alternate-universe Pronto Pizza & Beer. The layout of the two restaurants is basically the same, though PP remains level with the street instead of sloping down toward Hades. The elevation is not the only difference; the two places are similarly laid out, but atmospherically they could not be any more divergent. I don't think I would have noticed the similarities that *did* exist if these places hadn't both been on the same block and had the same name.

At PP&B, there was a counter to the left with a surly Italian-American dude being a dick (in the best possible way) and a huge cooler full of beers. The space opened up into a bunch of seating in the back, and there were radio speakers playing New Jack Swing. The seats and tables were mismatched, and the walls were almost entirely mirrored save for that Italian-flag molding. At plain old PP (though it wasn't actually sans B), there was a counter to the left with another damn cooler full of beers, but it was a little smaller than the cooler at PP&B. Behind the counter was a demure Middle Eastern gentleman, and he was super nice. The space opened up in the back, and there were all these tables and a bunch of weirdos hanging around; instead of a radio playing music there were multiple TVs showing a cable-access news channel, though the sound was only coming out of the TV located farthest in the back. The walls were orange instead of green, the tiles were brick-red instead of a neutral off-white, and the room was lined with many arched-window-shaped mirrors rather than one continuous mirror. Imagine taking PP&B and redecorating it to look like a Moroccan restaurant without changing the menu. One distinct commonality: there were destitute-looking men sleeping in the back of both places, though many of them seemed to be eating food from Indus Express.

The real distinguishing factor between PP and PP&B was that PP had even worse pizza than its predecessor. How could that be possible? The slice had virtually no sauce. The cheese— bland, white, lacking any subtlety or flavor—was the Drew Carey of dairy products. And the dough was vaguely reminiscent of angel food cake. Nate characterized it as "like a shitty biscuit."

As the three of us went bite for bite finishing it off (you know, so as not to be wasteful), I could see a pall descending over my companions. To a normal person, a bad slice of pizza can be just as disheartening as a good slice is uplifting, but I had been eating bad pizza for so long that I had developed something of a psychic callus. I was worried about my friends, though. They looked miserable. I asked how the slice made them feel. Cory said it made him feel sad. Nate said he felt ashamed. Calloused or not, I was starting to feel the effect of their low mo- rale. What was I doing eating all this pizza? What was the point? But then I looked down at my notebook for the next place and allowed myself to get a little excited.

It was located around the corner and was listed in my notes as Mondo Pizza—the word "Mondo" being richly evocative of my childhood in the late eighties and early nineties. I imagined the place looking like the Peach Pit or the Max, all Day-Glo colors and checkerboard floors, with a kindly, avuncular dude behind the counter dishing out advice alongside the slices.

"I bet the sign is gonna be, like, a black-and-white-checkered ska pattern with neon letters on it in that font that looks like written lightning bolts," I told the guys.

"No way!" Cory interrupted. "There's gonna be a dog wearing Oakleys and a backward hat scarfing a slice of pizza, and it'll say 'MONDO PIZZA' in all caps underneath."

Nate said, "Not at all. It's gonna be a plain white sign with 'Mondo' written in simple type, but the first *O* is gonna be a globe." (As it happens, "mondo" is Italian for "world," though I'm surprised Nate knew this.)

As we neared the place, we could see the sign hanging perpendicular to the building farther down the sidewalk. Sure enough, there was a globe, with a partial ring attaching it to the *M*, and both *O*s were pizza pies—one pepperoni, one plain. Why didn't we think of that?

But then as we got closer, we realized that this beautiful sign seemed to be the only thing that remained of Mondo Pizza. Instead, the awning above the storefront said "Michelle's Restaurant," and though there were no customers in sight, we could see a pizza oven through the window, so it was with no small amount of trepidation that we walked inside.

The restaurant had high ceilings and was brightly lit, like a Chinese Super Buffet, and the interior looked like mashed potatoes, all smudged white paint and light brown tabletops. The sole human presence was an old man sitting behind a folding table with a cash register perched on top of it. He wore a white shirt, a gold chain, and a white apron, and he had white hair and a small, wide face with kind if beleaguered eyes. In trying to remember his face, I keep seeing the wrinkled visage of the dwarf in the Black Lodge in *Twin Peaks*. He stared at us like an aging basset hound, equal parts inquisitive, forlorn, and resigned as he watched us eye the steam trays full of pasta, meat, and dumplings that looked as ancient as their guardian. There was no music playing, but the proprietor's quiet desperation was almost audible. Just as at Pizza Palace, stepping into Michelle's Restaurant felt like stepping outside of time. Not all pizza parlors are magical spaces, but the frequency with which they exude this sense of mystical atemporality is far greater than that of any other type of businesses I'm aware of.

Michelle's didn't have the same warmth as Pizza Palace, though. There was distrust hanging in the air. It felt as if we'd left Midtown and entered some Soviet-bloc village. A Soviet-bloc village with an ancient gas-fired pizza oven.

The old man silently offered up our slice, and we sat down at one of the empty tables in his desolate restaurant, unable to avoid his persistent gaze. He seemed to be watching us simply because there was nothing else to do.

But the slice . . . it was good! Maybe the best I had in that entire section of Midtown, an otherwise dead zone of disgusting pizza and sad business-attired automatons. This slice, while not the most incredible piece of pizza in the world, was expertly assembled. It contained a delicate balance of flavors—just enough salt in the dough, a hint of tang in the sauce. The texture of the crust was fantastic, the greasy, crunchy exterior giving way to soft, airy dough with each bite. It lacked that certain intangible something that makes a slice perfect; maybe there was no love in the food here, but otherwise it was as good as a slice can get. We took our time eating it, savoring every bite and dreading our return to the mean streets of Midtown.

"I think I'm getting serious with a girl," I told my friends, mouth full of food, as I passed the slice to Cory.

Nate arched his eyebrows. Cory was excited for me. "That lady with the shaved head you were with at the bar the other night?" he said. "Total babe."

"Right? I really like her. I think she might be the coolest person I know."

"So is she, like, your girlfriend?" Nate asked.

"I don't know. I mean, we haven't talked about it yet, and I don't even know how I feel about that stuff, but hopefully maybe she will be one day!"

"Yeah, dude. She's awesome." Cory shook his head ruminatively, chewing. "Does she have any friends?"

It seemed fitting that the slice at Michelle's would bring up happy thoughts—thoughts of Christina, her lovely stubbled head, and, perhaps, my future as her boyfriend. Maybe this day—and my life—was about to take a turn for the better. After our leisurely slice at Michelle's, we headed south to Forty-Fifth Street between Fifth and Sixth Avenues, a block that purported to contain four pizza parlors, the most of any block I had walked to date. It was a period of abundance. It was spring. We were feeling rejuvenated.

We had no idea how difficult it would be to make it from one end of that block to the other.

If, in the future, after Godzilla returns to rightfully reclaim the earth and humans are driven underground, where they live for centuries, slowly losing track of their history and humanity like in that one movie about dragons with Matthew McConaughey, but then eventually the dinosaurs all die from smoking too much weed and humans start to venture out and try to cobble civilization back together from the ruins and the only things that remain from the past are a few charred and frayed copies of *Slice Harvester* magazine and I am heralded as some kind of prophet or god figure, Nate Stark will be exalted as a saint.

When Nate, Cory, and I turned the corner onto Forty-Fifth Street from Fifth Avenue we were immediately confronted by Ambrosia, a horrid-looking cafeteria with the word "PIZZA" blinking deviously in neon through the window like the sign for a brothel in a Bolaño novel or a cat's eyes at night.

"Let's skip this place," was my suggestion.

"Yeah, fuck it." Cory was in.

Nate tried to interject, "No, guys, let's go. We gotta do it!"

Cory and I had already begun to stroll on. We literally could not stomach the idea of another sad, unremarkable Midtown slice after the brief reprieve we had just enjoyed at Michelle's. That was when the universe decided to fuck with us.

The next place we passed, two storefronts down, was called Milk N' Honey and was a Kosher pizza parlor. Across the street we noticed Metro Market Deli, another not-pizza place with another huge neon pizza sign. We had entered the little-known Tenth Circle of Hell. I suggested to everyone that we just skip this block and I would return to do it next week on my own as penance for all those Dylan Thomas poems I read to Christina's voice mail last week. But Nate was steadfast in his commitment to Harvesting. He just turned around and walked into Ambrosia muttering, "Well, *I'm* gonna get a slice." Cory and I followed obediently. Nate had inadvertently become our Virgil.

If the storefronts that line the Pronto Pizza block of West Forty-Eighth Street were evocative of a dystopian future city, then the inside of Ambrosia was like the food court on the space shuttle the rich people will be on when they evacuate Earth. The walls are lined with labeled ethnic food stalls—Pizza, Sushi, Mexican Food, Bagels—each festively decorated and displaying their mediocre foodstuffs as enticingly as possible. I have mentally labeled the center of the room Fancy Snack Island, a tiered construction offering up various confections as well as an assortment of healthy future-food bars containing special nutrients designed specifically for women, teens, or the elderly.

On the day we arrived there seemed to be delegations of tourists from a selection of church groups, all wearing matching T-shirts and talking excitedly and too loudly over the K-Pop on the radio. The pizza was being slung at the far back, so we had to walk an extra thirty feet just to get this terrible slice. It was overcooked and so dry that there may as well have been tumbleweeds rolling down my tongue when I bit into it. The dough was too thick, the sauce had no personality, and the cheese was the texture of semisoft plastic. "Ambrosia" means "food of the gods," which this slice was not. And it was just the beginning.

The next stop in the Tenth Circle was Milk N' Honey, the kosher fast-food joint two doors down. Now that Nate had assumed the role of Moses in the desert, we were about to suffer like some real Jews.

(I am the child of a lapsed Jew and a lapsed Catholic, though I feel my roots lie more within the secular Jewish intellectualism that dates back to the 1800s than with any kind of American Irish-Catholic identity. I grew up in a very Jewish place, and I have known some orthodox Jews in my life. I have been to synagogue a lot, attended a lot of Bar and Bat Mitzvahs, and seen a few foreskins get cut. My family has a Seder every year for Passover, when we talk about how the story of Passover relates to the plight of oppressed peoples worldwide. We mumble through a lot of the Hebrew but sing goofy songs in English. For the past few years my dad has tried to read the same really long e-mail forward that's a parody of "Who's on First." You get it— Cultural Jews, Ethnic Jews. We're even lower than Reform. They might have female rabbis, but at least they have rabbis! The point is, I feel a certain link to *Jewishness* if not *Judaism*, and yet there is an incredible distance between myself and the gray-bearded, mystical-looking old men and the fancy, wig-wearing ladies surrounded by children who sat in Milk N' Honey.)

I stood there that day and silently cursed Nate for bringing me across this threshold. I didn't understand these people, with their adherence to traditions and their easily articulated ethos. And they didn't understand me, with my weird tattoos and general antiauthoritarian surliness. Yet, I realized, we were linked in a number of inextricable ways. From Joey Ramone's ethnic identity to the fact that we are both weird separatist communities, there are many parallels between punks and Jews. Cory knows—Cory is Jewish in a weird, nonreligious way, too. Nate's *goy*, though. I know what you're thinking: "A *goy* from Berkeley? Poor guy can't catch a break." And you're right.

But all of the theoretical linkages between Punx and Jewz in the world couldn't change the fact that when we walked into Milk N' Honey I felt like an alien. And it didn't help that everyone basically stopped eating to stare at us, jaws agape, the entire time we ate our pizza, which, no surprise, wasn't very good, though it wasn't bad for a kosher slice. Nate said he liked it, but I think he was just afraid that any criticism on his part might be misconstrued as anti-Semitic.

After we finished eating I strolled over to the register to pay and a guy in a suit, who I assume was the owner, looked me up and down. "So, vhat did you tink of the slice?"

I gave him the High Brow, a shoulder shrug, and the most noncommittal "Wasn't bad" that I could muster. I mean, I didn't want to hurt the guy's feelings.

And you know what he did? He looked me straight in the face and said, "How good can it be? It's just pizza."

This man and I could not have been more different.

After Milk N' Honey, we crossed the street to eat another slice of total garbage pizza at Metro Market Deli, a crummier, more soulless version of Ambrosia, which at least had some character, even if the pizza sucked. There is an abundance of these terrible places in neighborhoods that are more commercial than residential. Something about corporate business districts enables the proliferation of these totally barren spaces that serve utilitarian *Blade Runner* cuisine. Nihilist food. "Might as well be a pill" food.

The pizza here was junk. It was tiny, it had no sauce, and the cheese felt synthetic. The dough was gritty and seemed more appropriate for exfoliating my athlete's foot than for eating. This pizza tasted like it came from somewhere outside New York, like some terrible road pizza you get on tour in Northern California or western Pennsylvania. It was disgusting and not worth it, but I'm glad we ate it, because if we hadn't, we'd be left to wonder how bad a slice of pizza could truly be.

Our final destination on Forty-Fifth Street (though only our penultimate destination for the day's pizza mission) was a place called The World Famous Little Italy Pizza (say that five times fast), and it was the only *actual* pizzeria of the four pizza-serving establishments on the block. We were fooled into thinking that perhaps this place might be decent, and therein lay its danger.

The air inside The World Famous Little Italy Pizza was thick and humid, like that of a tropical rain forest. There was a leak in the ceiling and some busted-ass steampunk light fixtures that looked like the décor on an airship in one of the PlayStation Final Fantasy games. The front of the restaurant held a few crummy tables, and there was a narrow hallway leading to the too-bright back, where it opens up into a pizza counter. The good thing about this place is that you can just walk in here and sit and read for, like, an hour, and it's a pain in the ass for the employees to come tell you to leave because they're all the way in the back. The bad thing about it is everything else.

When we walked in, Nate and Cory secured an empty table while I went to the back to organize a slice. I walked up to the counter and surveyed the scene. A smattering of pies sat behind Plexiglas, none of them looking spectacular but none of them looking downright bad, either. Maybe this place was gonna be okay after all. I asked the cool teenage slacker working there for a plain slice.

"There's a fresh pie coming out in a second," he told me, paying more attention to his phone than to my order.

I let him know that I didn't mind if he had to reheat one. "I actually prefer it," I told him.

He just shook his head. "No slices left. Fresh pie in a few minutes."

This was possibly a first for me: being in a pizza place that didn't actually have a plain pizza sliced and ready to reheat. I tried to convince myself that maybe The World Famous Little Italy Pizza was so good, so popular, that they could barely keep up. But then I looked around the empty restaurant, recalled that no one had entered or left in the ten minutes since I'd wandered in off the street, and realized that these people were just lazy. Okay, more power to 'em! As a former lazy employee, I stand in solidarity with slackers and layabouts worldwide, even when it slightly inconveniences me.

I was starting to worry about getting a fresh pie because I wanted to like this place, and sometimes fresh pies aren't crunchy enough for my tastes. A good pizza place knows how to do it, but at your average shlock joint they partially cook the slicing pies during the slow times of day so that they won't burn when reheating. I was scared this slice might be well prepared but undercooked. My fear wound up being groundless, though, because the slice this guy handed me was totally incinerated. Just burnt to a fucking crisp.

The cheese was burnt to the point that it didn't have flavor, only the terrible texture of a rubber spatula. The sauce was a sick paste that made the whole slice taste like the minestrone soup my friend Matt Birdflu used to buy me with his California food stamps from the dollar store across the street from the West Oakland BART station: deeply entrenched in a culture of high fructose corn syrup and bad vibes. Biting into the crust was a troubling experience.

Looking introspective, Cory said, "You know that part of *Demolition Man* where Sylvester Stallone freezes Wesley Snipes with liquid nitrogen and then smashes him up with a hammer or whatever?"

Nate and I both nodded our heads in the affirmative.

"When I bite this crust, it feels like that's happening in my mouth."

Having made it through the perpetually worsening punishment that is the pizza parlors of Forty-Fifth Street, we felt a certain sense of invulnerability. We strode through Midtown like a gang, blustering and powerful. In the face of an obstacle so great we nearly folded (aka Ambrosia), we'd fought on and found a source of strength within ourselves we hadn't known we possessed.

We had one more stop on our day's excursion, and in line with the weird theme of the afternoon, it was called The World Famous Little Italy, one word away from the name of the place we'd eaten at beforehand, although this place was around the corner rather than on the same exact block, as with PP and PP&B.

The first thing we saw, before we even walked into the place, was a three-foot-tall sign in the window proclaiming that The World Famous Little Italy is an independent, autonomous entity with no affiliations:

To Our Customers:

Little Italy Pizza

Has

ALWAYS Been our

ONLY Location and

NOT Affiliated with

any other Little Italy.

Thanks and Have

A Fantabulous Day.

The Management

The sign itself was etched into a piece of metal, an affordable approximation of stone. Basically this thing was, like, commandment status. In no uncertain terms, they wanted you to know they had nothing to do with that shithole around the corner. Surrounding the sign were "artifact" ceramics and weird-shaped glass bottles full of olives, a classic example of the Olive Garden school of rustic, Tuscan décor.

There were no seats in the place and, like, four hundred employees jammed behind the small counter. The back wall was fake marble and sported a mural of a horse hanging out in some cobblestone alley surrounded by family crests, shields, and other olden-tymes paraphernalia rendered in muted, "distressed" earth tones attempting to evoke a sense of being Back in the Day but actually revealing themselves as woefully contemporary.

If this were the movies, the next slice of pizza would be the best slice I'd ever had. Its delicately flavored sauce would meld seamlessly with hot, gooey cheese, and it would all rest atop a slightly salty, perfectly crunchy, doughy foundation. In the movies I'd eat the slice, and everything would turn around. My life wouldn't feel so stale; I'd find my purpose. Maybe I'd befriend the pizza man and become his apprentice. I'd learn the trade and strike out to open up a pizzeria of my own.

Well, this ain't the movies, kid.

The slice at The World Famous Little Italy was totally dead center, middle of the road—neither particularly good nor particularly bad. If we lived in a better world, this would be the worst that pizza ever got, and then things would incrementally get better until we found my holy grail, the perfect slice.

The good news is, the best slice wasn't far away. But Forty-Fifth Street had chewed me up and spit me out the way I might've done to the pizza at Ambrosia if I wasn't too PC to waste food, and I was left unresolved. Probably I went to the bar that night and drank myself into oblivion. Likely I recited morbid poetry into my not-quite-girlfriend's voice mail. Slice Harvester, which had once been my anchor, was no longer working. What's a boy to do when he can't even believe in pizza anymore?

CHAPTER 7

Hell's Kitchen Pizza

Sadly, this pizza is the worst pizza I've had in my entire life. It was so bad that after I took my first bite, I felt like I was gonna puke. Caroline took a bite, gagged, spit it into a napkin, and said, "I eat out of the trash pretty regularly, and I don't have this problem."

—*Slice Harvester Quarterly*, Issue 4, "Forty-Second to Fifty-Ninth Streets," visited May 22, 2010

Opposite page: A pigeon, feasting

One hundred eighty-eight slices since I'd started Harvesting, and it was one of those nights. I was working the five-to-eleven shift at the burrito restaurant in the pouring rain bringing seitan chorizo enchiladas to lazy yuppies who didn't tip. The new bartender at the restaurant had a policy that entitled the delivery guys to free whiskey whenever it was cold or raining and the owner wasn't looking, so I was working on a solid, sustainable drunk by about eight p.m., biking around without a care in the world. Sometimes I would get a credit card order where I could see the tip was bad and I'd reach into my basket and mush the food up with my hand, but otherwise I didn't have a bitter thought for anyone—not the cars throwing their doors open in front of my bike, not the women pushing their baby strollers out into the street. None of it could bother me. It was a picturesquely rainy spring evening and I was drunk, and I had a cool new girlfriend and people really seemed to like my new zine and I had friends from the Northwest in town visiting and I was meeting them at the bar after work.

With the help of a half dozen shots of whiskey and a few beers, my six-hour shift flew by in what seemed like a matter of minutes. I ate a quesadilla, smoked a cigarette, and headed to the bar to meet my friends from over yonder. I'm certain we drank whiskey. I'm certain we all hugged and clinked glasses at some point, talked about punk stuff, asked after mutual friends, and made plans to travel to one another that we all knew no one would follow through on but that felt nice to make. I'm certain I felt very happy. I'm certain that I drank to the point where it felt like I was being carried through the room on the wings of an angel. I know that I stayed out way too late drinking and reveling, but what's the point of being alive if you don't spend any time *living*, right?

The next morning I was meeting Caroline and her sister to go eat some pizza around Forty-Second Street in Hell's Kitchen. And when I say morning, I mean two p.m. the next afternoon. I have no compunction about sleeping through the day. Maybe it's important if you're part of the square world and need to go to an office job, but as I'm sure you know by now, I do not. When I woke up at 12:30 on my mattress on the floor and bulldozed through my sloppy apartment to the bathroom for my morning puke, I had barely enough energy to text Caroline and her sister to ask them if we could meet an hour later than planned. I puked again, drank a little bit of water, and went back to sleep until 2:30.

While the morning puke had become something of a norm for me at this point in my life, I understand that perhaps not everyone can comprehend such an existence. The human body's adaptability to uncomfortable situations is one of the evolutionary traits that have kept us successfully out of the jaws of extinction. Think about the countless cultures that have flourished in extreme climates and barren wastelands. And since then, at least in the first world, technology has advanced to the point where adversity is rarely so extreme, so this inherent trait has been deflected toward other, less-urgent obstacles. People in Pennsylvania, for instance, think the pizza in Pennsylvania is good. This is not because the pizza in Pennsylvania is actually good pizza—it's because the average American teen can't survive without ready access to good pizza, and so the minds of Pennsylvanians are necessarily warped from childhood as a survival tactic. Similarly, I had puked on so many mornings for so many years that my body was inured to it. It was just something I did.

I guess the groundwork for my acceptance of such a life was laid when I was nineteen or twenty. I was sitting in this weird café in New Orleans with my friend Tony, telling him about the new apartment I had just rented. I was complaining about the small bathroom, and he said, "I love a small bathroom. It's really important to have a space where you can puke into the sink or tub while you're sitting on the toilet shitting. For hangovers."

I was shocked. "I hope I'm never that hungover in my life."

"What are you talking about, man? Hangovers are great—probably one of the most life-affirming experiences there is. It feels like shit is gonna suck forever and you want to give up for good, but if you force yourself out of bed and go about your day, first you get used to it, and then eventually it ends. And, seriously, if you just pretend feeling like shit is awesome, then it actually doesn't suck." Tony had a way with words.

Within a few years I was more or less living by these words, and on this particular spring afternoon, sitting on the train heading into the city to meet my best friend and her sister, I was in the throes of just such an experience—looking around the subway feeling like a goon, worrying that *everyone knows*. Riding the subway with a terrible hangover is not dissimilar to riding the subway while waiting for the two hits of acid you just took to kick in. You're the only one wearing sunglasses and you think everyone is staring at you, and you feel an acute awareness that you are somehow So Different from all of them and an equally strong impulse to keep it a secret.

And the appeal of a hangover is not so different from the more triumphant aspects of the majority of my psychedelic experiences. The awesomeness of The Drunkenness or the Majorly Tripping Out is the precursor to the Real Intellectual Activity. Which is to say, the inevitable moment when you start to wonder, *Will this ever end? Have I finally doomed myself to an eternity of living like this? I have. I'm stuck like this forever. I may never recover. Shit.* You start scribbling an apology letter to your mom, stressing how you'll tie up all your loose ends. *Gotta find someone to take care of my cats before I go AWOL.* But it eventually does end. You return to normal cognitive lucidity, to absolutely regular human functioning.

The first time I ate mushrooms, at sixteen or seventeen, was in my friend Jason's apartment in a building that had been converted from a former elementary school. The 1970s decor in the hallways was reminiscent of *The Shining*, and his bedroom was in the clock tower, with the face of the clock transformed into a giant window, cobbled together out of bits of glass. Unlike my first acid experience, which was relatively anticlimactic, eating mushrooms felt incredibly revelatory. After I ran around the apartment pretending I was Spider-Man and climbing up and down everything that was climbable, I wandered outside barefoot and sat on a bench in the park with my feet in the snow and felt like it had been a fun time and I was glad it was over.

That's when I started hallucinating again. I grew very afraid that I was some special type of person on whom mushrooms work *too well* and that I was going to be stuck tripping FOREVER. I didn't know what to do; I was freaking out, my feet were getting cold, and I was locked outside. This was before cell phones, so I had to just frantically ring the buzzer and hope that someone would let me back in, but my friends inside were tripping, too, and I didn't know if they'd ever hear it and shit was getting *so dark*. (Not literally; it had gotten Literally Dark long ago, it being the middle of the night, but, like, things were getting Metaphysically Dark.) Eventually someone must have let me in, because my feet are still attached to my ankles as of this writing. I don't remember coming inside or the segue between shit feeling eternally fucked and shit feeling okay again; the next thing I remember is lying on Jason's bed, watching the sun creep through his weird window while smoking a joint and listening to Jimi Hendrix, feeling the swelling pride of a young man in possession of intimate knowledge. I knew that if I had gotten through that ordeal alive, I could face anything.

This is the important lesson about that first seminal psychedelic experience or major hangover, because it carries over to other parts of life, like your first bad breakup or the first time someone you love dies.

At twenty-three, I was on tour with an old band—this was before Jamie died, and he had canceled two weeks' worth of moving jobs and lent us his van for the tour. My cell phone had been dead for days, but I wasn't expecting anyone to call me, and besides, I was going to be home soon. My friend Kevin, whose band had squeezed into Jamie's windowless van with mine to take our decidedly derivative and banal punk rock to our friends and acquaintances down the East Coast, pulled his cell phone out of his pocket, listened for a few seconds, and handed the phone to me.

"Hello . . . ?"

My father was on the other end. I thought I could hear him laughing and wondered what kind of joke was so urgent that he'd spent god knows how long tracking down Kevin's number.

"Dad . . . ?"

Still laughing. I started trying to trace backward from Kevin's number to other people who knew other people who knew someone whose phone number my dad knew. This wasn't making any sense to me, and it was beginning to make me uncomfortable.

"How'd you get this number?"

I suddenly realized my father was crying, not laughing. I'd never heard him cry.

"Your uncle Scott . . ." he choked out. "Your uncle Scott . . . my baby brother . . . he had a heart attack. He was in the car with Mom. They'd pulled into a rest stop. If it had happened five minutes before or after, he would've been behind the wheel with her in the car, and she would've been dead, too."

I was on my way to the last show on my first tour playing a guitar my uncle had given me. My dad and I talked some more and decided I should play the show. I'd be home in two days. By the time I curled up in the back of the van sobbing, the seven other people traveling with me had overheard enough of the conversation to give me some space. I took my knife off my belt and carved "FUCK YOU" into the bottom of the guitar. Cory put a Kimya Dawson record on. I fell asleep.

When we got to DC, my friends Marcia and Alana were waiting for us. Someone had told them what was going on with me, and Marcia had already gotten a fifth of whiskey and a box of beers. I sat in the van slugging whiskey and pounding beers, and then went into the house long enough to play the show through my tears and to drunkenly try to fight someone who lived there. I was home the next day.

My family celebrates birthdays for a whole week, so it's fitting that we should celebrate funerals for a year. We had a family funeral and a friends funeral; we scattered the ashes; we buried the urn. All were separate occurrences, some months apart. None of them served to dull the indelible pain that comes with losing someone close. That year I got drunk and cried a lot, wrote one totally bullshit Social Distortion rip-off song about being sad, and listened to "Kiss The World Goodbye" by Kris Kristofferson every day. None of it worked to assuage my grief, but it distracted me. And then one day I wasn't living with the constant specter of my sadness anymore. Maybe I'd feel a tender moment when listening to a song or I'd have a dream where Scott and I went and ate ribs and he told me about where I was fucking my life up, but mostly I moved on. I didn't forget him by any means, but I was no longer fixated on his loss. It just became part of me.

And I guess what I'm saying is, every hangover is like a miniature run-through of the grief cycle. Every morning that I woke up feeling like the entire world was full of nothing but piss and shit, like I didn't deserve to see sunlight, like I was going to turn into a CHUD, led ultimately to a triumphant afternoon of overcoming the odds. Living most of my life in an intense fog put my moments of clarity into greater focus. It taught me to value lucidity, but not to rely on it.

That afternoon when I stepped off the subway into the misty spring air, I was in the eye of the storm—the part of the hangover where it fakes you out and you think it's over, so you start behaving like it's over (ingesting things besides water, standing upright, being more than ten feet from a bathroom), only to have it rear its ugly head once again, screaming "PSYCH! YOU THOUGHT YOU WERE SOME KINDA TOUGH GUY? YOU THOUGHT ALL OF A SUDDEN THAT EVEN THOUGH YOUR HANGOVERS HAVE LASTED MOST OF THE DAY FOR YEARS, YOU HAD ME BEATEN IN ONLY TWO HOURS? WELL, YOU DIDN'T! I TRICKED YOU!" Sadly, I was still an hour or two away from that startling discovery, and so I approached the world with unchecked optimism.

The first pizza parlor was a 99¢ Fresh dollar-slice joint on Forty-Second Street between Eighth and Ninth Avenues, on the outskirts of Times Square. A New York slice is an altogether different food from a traditional Neapolitan pie, in the same way an apple is different from a pear. One is a little more pedestrian, a little more blunt and rugged, while the other is subtler, more gourmet. Similarly, a New York slice is different from a dollar slice in the same way an apple is different from a bodega apple pie. The former may be common, pedestrian, but it is still real food, and in its simplicity lies its charm. The latter, while one can tell it was somehow derived from the former, has been abstracted to such a point that it belongs more in the realm of science than anything else. Which is to say, it exists in an entirely substandard milieu, though within that milieu there is a full spectrum of varying quality.

I was feeling subhuman that afternoon, though, so it felt

appropriate to be eating subpar pizza. And while this slice was destined to fail, it was appealing in its own way. We took our time eating, savoring the fast-food quality of the slice and the vibrant memories it conjured. I remembered adolescent Friday nights spent at the ice-skating rink. Leah called it "a carnival slice with a little dash of cafeteria." Caroline agreed that it was sentimentally pleasing, but to her health-conscious palate, it just tasted like massive amounts of corn syrup.

The bites of dollar slice having made me a little less wobbly, we set out to eat more pizza. We hit a handful of shlock joints (square slices; unremediable grossness; massive undercooking) and one actual pizzeria (Claudio Pizzeria on Tenth Avenue— good slice, great vibes) before we walked into what would be our final stop of the day, the possible nadir of my entire pizza-eating career. Hell's Kitchen Pizza, on Tenth Avenue up toward Fiftieth Street, serves, hands down, the worst pizza I've ever eaten in my life.

Now, the place was not without its charms. I am certainly fond of the mid-nineties White Zombie aesthetic. The mash-up of the heavy metal and psychobilly subcultures creates something so uniquely, guilelessly, and confidently corny that it almost moves straight past kitsch into the realm of cool. Paint everything black, and then paint flames on all of it and hang old Betty Page bondage pinups everywhere, and then play a live Springsteen album, and I am pretty much smitten. I know the combination is in objectively bad taste, but that doesn't matter to me. It reminds me of my adolescence, when I was a sort-of goth/sort-of punk/sort-of skater/generally unsatisfied little dude corndoggin' all over town, thinking I was the coolest. In eighth grade, I wore to school, earnestly believing I looked *fucking cool*, a pair of cropped JNCO jeans paired with combat boots with Day-Glo orange New Kids on the Block shoelaces I had stolen from a store on St. Marks Place and a T-shirt with the lyrics to the *Shaft* theme song, with my hair in four pigtails. I am neither proud nor ashamed of this legacy, but that was me trying to be me, and I will never scorn someone who presents himself in a similar fashion.

Anyway, no amount of cute décor could convince me to like the awful pizza in this wonderful place. Biting into the blobby cheese and mealy dough was unpleasant enough, but when the putrid flavor of the rotten sauce hit my tongue, I felt like I was gonna hurl—though to be fair and accurate in my reporting, the feeling quickly subsided. "Hell's Kitchen" is right—this pizza might have been prepared by Lucifer himself. Caroline actually spit her first bite into a napkin and said, "I eat out of the trash pretty regularly, and I don't have this problem." Leah seemed unfazed by the slice, but she didn't make any claims that it was good. She and I finished it, but Caroline had chosen to abstain from eating any more.

About half a block from Hell's Kitchen Pizza, Caroline and Leah noticed dozens of antique nails and plumbing fixtures sitting in a garbage can on the sidewalk and began to dig through to see if any of them were worth taking home. Suddenly, without warning, I was seized by an intense need to vomit. Perhaps my hangover had crept back up on me, but more likely my body had begun to digest the food I had just eaten and revolted before the poison could be fully assimilated into my system. Whatever the cause—residual hangover or repulsive pizza—I managed to make my way off the sidewalk and in between two parked luxury cars, which I leaned on as I barfed my brains out for a good seven minutes.

I looked up between heaves to see a few Yuppie Moms pushing their Beautiful Aryan Babies down the street. When they saw Caroline and Leah digging through the trash, they looked somewhat aghast. When they noticed me in the gutter (where I belong) puking my guts out, they grew alarmed and chose to cross the street rather than pass through the Dirtbag Strait of Messina that the three of us had transformed our portion of the sidewalk into.

I was still a bit dizzy when my puking subsided, so I sat down on the curb to roll a cigarette. As I lit my smoke and regained my vision, a family of birds alighted upon my puke puddle and began to sup. They chirped to one another as they ate the food I had just expelled, probably talking about some other meal that they had recently eaten, which is what my family always talks about when we eat.

"This puke is good; what do you think it is?" chirps Baby Bird.

"Maybe a can of Spaghetti-Os and a piece of white bread?" his father chirps back.

Mama bird chimes in, "Tastes like pizza to me."

This excites Papa Bird. "Remember that pizza we found in the phone booth on Thirty-Eighth Street?" he asks, his eyes glazing over with fond memories.

"Oh boy, do I!" Baby Bird interjects.

"Much better than this pizza we're eating right now," says Mama Bird definitively.

And so on.

After my Slice Harvest with Caroline and Leah, I had an hour to kill before meeting my friend Milo after he got out of work, so I decided to sit in a park and read my Samuel Delany novel. I looked forward to it. Sitting and reading in parks has been a favorite activity of mine since I was a teenager, when I would perch on a bench with a Kerouac novel or a book of Rilke poems angled conspicuously so that passersby might see how cool I was. I sat and stared at garbage prose and poetry in the hopes that someone interesting would start a conversation with me about it and I could say something precocious. These days I care far more about what I'm reading than what people will think of what I'm reading. I like to read outside, because it's a true test of a good book. If it can draw me in despite the myriad distractions and stimuli available outdoors in Manhattan at any given moment, it's definitely worth my time. A block from the park it started pouring rain, so I ducked into a McDonald's where I knew I could sit anonymously and read undisturbed for an hour.

Ten pages into my chapter, I was yanked out of the elaborate civilization that Delany had carefully crafted for me by a cacophony of screams. I looked up and saw a solitary gentleman wearing nothing but a pair of forest-green sweatpants and an NYPD baseball cap berating everyone who was trying to walk out of the fast-food store—another Ghost of Christmas Future. He was a bedraggled man of about fifty, though he may have only been a haggard thirty for all I knew. He stood in the doorway like a defensive lineman on a football field, screaming "CAN ANYONE TELL

ME WHERE THE UNITED STATES OF AMERICA ARE?" or "I WORK FOR THE CITY!" at no one in particular while pointing at the acronym embroidered on his hat. I felt an overwhelming sympathy for him. I wanted to give him a sweatshirt and something warm to eat, maybe walk him over to Callen Lorde Community Health Center for a psychiatric evaluation. But more than that, I felt terror for myself. This man was the embodiment of all my deepest fears. I felt like I was only a few poor choices, a few slight missteps away from myself standing barefoot, shouting at strangers in the foyer of a McDonald's. He brought together all of the fears that came with every hangover, which I tried to stave off with varying degrees of success. I'm sure this man hadn't always been such a wreck. But he had Gone There one day and never came back.

I spent the next forty minutes trying to pay attention to my book through the racket. No one in the McDonald's made even the slightest attempt to eject him, and no one walking by engaged him. Everyone ignored him. Here he was, making a spectacle of himself but remaining entirely invisible at the same time—the ultimate magician's illusion. As I packed my bag and got ready to leave, I steeled myself for confrontation, wondering whether I would say anything, if I would try to have a conversation. As I approached the door, I watched the man lean over to scream his desperate question into the face of a child of no more than ten, who didn't even bat an eye. I watched him turn around and holler in the face of a biker walking in the door. He swiveled again when he heard my footsteps approaching, looked me up and down, smiled, and gave me a nod that said, "Hey, brother," as if he knew me. I nodded back.

So many moments happened that could've been my bottom

but weren't. The time I ate half a dozen Klonopins because I was so drunk I kept forgetting I had taken one already and then took some mystery pill, I think maybe methadone, that I had traded my neighbor a beer for; the time I was biking around, drunk out of my mind, wearing headphones and running red lights, and then an SUV driver slammed on his brakes and barely didn't hit me, and the only reason he hit those brakes in time was because he heard me screaming along to the chorus of "It's Late" by Queen before he ever saw me; any of the times I ended up in the hospital from wrecking my bike while drunk; driving drunk home from Jamie's funeral because I had to do eight hundred shots at the shitty Long Island biker bar next door before I could cry; puking in the bathroom at my grandma's tiny apartment on Thanksgiving morning while my mom was having a meltdown because she was watching her own mother die slowly before her eyes and she was powerless in the face of it, and instead of being there for her I was sweating like crazy, hoping she was too distraught and distracted to notice. And even all those moments are pretty PG-13 for the real rock bottoms we've all seen in TV and movies. Hell, those moments are PG-13 compared to those some of the shit friends of mine who *still* drink and do drugs have made it through unfazed.

As enticing as it is for narrative purposes to try to find a bottom to refer to, there just isn't one. (If you ever hear me mention "my bottom," you can rest assured I'm only talking about the butt in my pants.) My alcoholism, which continued well past the moment when I finally recognized it, was far more mundane than that. Luckily, I found my way up and out eventually—thanks in part to my Pizza Quest, which had, at this point, actually hit bottom.

Awarded
"One of the 10
BEST PIZZAS IN N.Y.C."

Ny Pizza Suprema

CHAPTER 8

Blue Rose Deli

Pizza like this is ruining America. Well, pizza like this and Walmart and the Religious Right and the Prison-Industrial Complex and the Military-Industrial Complex and on and on and on. Fuck it—America was ruined from the get-go, but at least New York's all right, and this pizza is ruining New York.

—*Slice Harvester Quarterly*, Issue 5, "Twenty-Third to Forty-Second Streets," visited on May 26, 2010

Opposite page: Pizza Suprema, 413 Eighth Avenue

Leaving the McDonald's, I walked over to Times Square to pick up Milo from the patent office so I could borrow a hundred dollars to take Tina out for our three-month anniversary. ("Tina" is an abbreviation for "Christina," as if you didn't figure that out.) Milo and I have been friends since we were thirteen. And in the community of Punk, which is just as much a family as it is a gang, Milo is my Better Twin. We have very similar mannerisms, though he is generally more successful and productive than I am, and more capable of dealing with the intricacies of life. He's an Actual Mathematician with a degree from MIT, who works as a patent agent and has managed to hold the same cool-ass job for the past decade despite living in wild punk houses and partying relentlessly for years, whereas I'm a "writer" who dropped out of college and has been fired from or quit a string of service jobs. Milo is a man who has only one flaw, and you won't believe what it is: he doesn't like pizza.

He would certainly not agree with that self-deprecating assessment, of course, and nor do I, at least not always. But that's how it feels sometimes, and that's definitely how it felt when I was meeting him to borrow a hundred bucks to take my girlfriend out to dinner.

Anyway, after meeting Milo, I dipped into some shitty

Irish pub and had two shots of well whiskey in quick succession before getting on the train. I went home and tried to read, dozed off, and suddenly awoke with the realization that I was running the risk of being late for dinner. And I hadn't gotten flowers yet! I checked my phone—Tina hadn't called. There was still time.

I threw on my clothes and jumped on my bike. All the flower shops were closed, but after a quick rummage in the garbage bags out front I had a basket full of flowers. Dumpster flowers are cooler anyway. I arranged them into a series of bouquets tied together with shredded plastic and ducked into a bar. I got a shot and a beer, drank the shot right away, and was taking my first sip of beer when my phone buzzed with a text from Tina.

off the train

I slammed the rest of my beer, ran outside, hopped on my bike, and sprinted toward the subway. As I got closer, I pulled out a couple of tulips and held them in one hand, so that when Tina spotted me she'd see my raggedy ass on my raggedy-ass bike holding out some raggedy-ass trash flowers, and if she didn't think I was the best boyfriend, she would be crazy.

I took her to the fancy French restaurant in my neighborhood that I always thought was for yuppies, but it turned out to be really good. Romantic dinner ahoy! I ordered us a bottle of wine and some escargot, which Christina had never eaten before. She got the coq au vin and I got a steak, and we ate and drank and looked into each other's eyes, and everyone was in love and the world was okay.

We finished our entrees and ordered dessert. As the waiter was leaving, I filled up my wineglass and realized the carafe was empty. I looked up at Christina with a mischievous glint in my eye. "Should we get another bottle?"

She didn't say anything at first. I thought maybe she didn't hear me over the other customers and the music and the rapturous delight of eating such a fine meal with such an awesome dude. But then she answered coldly, "Do whatever you want."

I couldn't understand what was going on. We were supposed to be having a romantic dinner. We were pretending to be normal, square adults celebrating an anniversary, and it was supposed to be fun and silly, and why was she acting like this? I was starting to panic, as I am apt to do. "What's wrong?" I asked a little too loudly.

"I'm still on my first glass, Colin," she said, her voice flat and sterile. "You drank the whole bottle yourself."

"So we won't get another one! No big deal. We'll eat some dessert, have an espresso, and then go get a nightcap at the bar. Or we can just go home. I don't care! We don't need more wine. I'm sorry I'm drinking so fast! I'm nervous. I don't need to drink anymore."

"It's not just the wine, Colin. You're drunk all the time. You puke every morning. I think you have a problem."

I was furious. "How dare you! This is ridiculous. I might drink a lot, but I don't miss work, and I keep up with Slice Harvester. I'm fine. I think you're the one with the problem," I shouted.

Dessert arrived, punctuating my angry outburst. Tina got up, put on her coat, and left the restaurant. I finished our crème brûlée in silence, paid the bill, and went to the bar alone.

The day after Tina's and my failed date night, I was scheduled to eat pizza with my friend Jonathan Tesnakis, a great writer from Staten Island who lives in San Francisco. I wanted to cancel because I was hungover and sad. Slice Harvesting wasn't gonna fix things with Tina, but I realized that if I stayed at home, I would get drunk, watch *Valley Girl*, and then listen to "Another Girl, Another Planet" on repeat till I cried myself to sleep. I decided that it would be better for everyone if I actually did what I was supposed to do instead of lying around feeling sorry for myself like a big whiny baby. So I trooped into the city and met up with Jonathan.

It was good that I went, because we ended up eating at what was one of my favorite pizza places, and it really helped me dig my way out of the funk I had put myself in. Siena Pizza is a totally nondescript storefront right across from the Port Authority. When meeting out-of-town friends who arrive by bus, it's often the first place I'll take them. The slice isn't perfect, but it's pretty damn close, and it's nice to fill yourself up with the loving warmth of New York City first thing upon arrival.

When I was nineteen, I spent a week in Baltimore hanging out with these totally rugged, White Rasta gangbangers. I had spent time in that town as a young teenager and had always meant to go back, because it's so grimy and strange. In the summer of 2002 this guy Doug, whom I smoked weed with, mentioned that he was going home to Baltimore, and I don't remember whether I invited myself or he invited me, but we both went back to see his crew. They were these totally wild boys, small-time criminals, living crazy lives on the outskirts of town. This was toward the end of my teenage all-day-every-day weed smoking years, so I was still puffing hella blunts, but it was starting to wear me out and make me miserable. I think that Sunday morning in Baltimore when all those thugs got me stoned and then had a White Rasta bible discussion was the last time I ever felt comfortable being high around strangers.

I was grateful to have been afforded the opportunity to observe someone else's weird life for that week, but I was really glad to go back to NYC. I ended up walking from Doug's parents' house to the bus station in downtown Baltimore. About halfway there a downpour started, a fitting end to a strange week for sure, but I spent the whole bus ride shivering under the air conditioner, soaked to the bone.

As soon as I got off the bus I practically ran out of Port Authority and made a beeline for Siena. That slice hit the spot so perfectly. When I munched that incredible pizza and felt its warmth spread throughout my body, I knew things were going to be different from now on. I had changed somehow, but I was safe, and I was home. Sure enough, I more or less stopped smoking weed after that.

My slice with Jonathan was just as good as the one I remembered. Heading home that day, I thought about the cycles my life had taken: smoking weed all the time in high school until I more or less quit when I was nineteen, at which point I started getting drunk pretty regularly. Maybe it was time for that to end, too.

A few days later I sucked it up and apologized to Christina for acting like such a baby, acknowledged that she was right about my drinking being problematic, and promptly began to lie constantly about where I was and what I was doing in order to avoid having to actually change my bummer lifestyle. This, dear reader, is what we call "being proactive."

Sometimes lying can be fun and harmless, like when you tell some lady who picks you up while hitchhiking that your parents are Orthodox Jews and your dad owns a Food Lion outside Louisville and your mom is a cantor at one of the only synagogues in the area, and that you went to high school in New Jersey, where you lived with your aunt and uncle while your parents were going through an ugly divorce because your mom cheated on your dad with the rabbi, and that's why you don't have a southern accent. The point is, I may have done that once or twice. But up until the aftermath of the dinner debacle with Tina, I had never lied about anything serious or lied to a partner.

It's fucked-up how easy it turned out to be. The more I lied, the more natural it became. And the more I lied, the more lies I had to tell. What started as a simple act of deception suddenly became a labyrinth. I was King Minos, and my drinking was the Minotaur that I was desperately trying to hide. It started out with little things. If Tina and I went out for a drink together and she went to the bathroom, I would quickly order a round of shots for us and then drink both of them before she got back. If we were sitting at a table with friends, I would always offer to go up and buy the next round, because that way I could secretly slam a whiskey without anyone noticing.

I did honestly curtail my drinking, because I realized I couldn't be puking in the morning when Tina and I slept in the same bed. To make up for it, on the nights we weren't together, I would rage twice as hard. When I realized that I couldn't call her to say good night at seven a.m. when I was leaving the bar, I started waiting to go to the bar until after she had gone to sleep, or leaving the bar for ten minutes, going to my quiet house to call and pretend that I was going to sleep at two or three, and then going back to the bar. These were little things, but they added up.

Eventually I started spending so much time at the bar that they asked me if I wanted to work there. It was a definite step up from being a delivery boy—easily twice as much pay, I got to work indoors, and I was *expected* to drink at work (!!!)— but I knew Tina would never approve of my working there. This problem had an easy solution: I just didn't tell her. Technically, I never lied about it. I told her I was working different days and that my hours had changed, which was the truth; I just happened to never mention that my *job* had changed as well. I talked around it. When she asked how work had been, I gave noncommittal, one-word answers. I described interactions with customers but implied that they were people I was delivering food to, though I never said it outright. I left a space for her to fill in with the knowledge that she already had, and I convinced myself that it was okay, because though I wasn't being honest, I wasn't exactly being *dishonest*, either.

All this lying was really hard on me, and to cope with it, I started drinking *much* more. Not that I was getting drunker— I had actually finally learned a modicum of self-control and had stopped blacking out every night. Instead, I began to stay slightly drunk for most of the day. I was never into beer for breakfast, but I quickly grew to love White Horse Scotch in my coffee. And I drank a lot of coffee. This lifestyle of constant anxiety coupled with slight drunkenness gave me heinous, consistent diarrhea. I'm sure it didn't help that I basically ate only pizza, Dumpstered bagels, and sardine sandwiches.

I made up for all this by being the best boyfriend ever when I wasn't lying about being drunk or doing drugs with strangers. I brought her flowers all the time. When her lease ran out I borrowed a friend's van and helped her move. When she lost her job at the burger restaurant I got her a job at the coffee shop my friend Johnny ran. I cooked her meals, I bought her groceries, I got her cute little presents from the dollar store or the thrift shop all the time. I ingratiated myself to her friends, so that if I ever got found out, they would hopefully convince her to stay with me. I built her a really cute bike. I got an old frame from Marcia and then spent weeks riding around at night with bike tools in my bag, lifting parts from the many obviously abandoned bikes cluttering up the telephone poles and parking meters of our fair city. I *may* have accidentally stolen some parts from some bikes that possibly weren't abandoned, but never anything big.

My behavior was clearly intolerable by any standard, but it is especially hypocritical for me because I spent the better part of my twenties working with Support New York, a punk political collective engaged in accountability work with accused sexual assaulters within the activist community. That's a really complicated sentence, maybe, but the gist of it is very simple: the tentacles of patriarchy have been codified in our judicial system to the point where it has become difficult for survivors of sexual violence to receive actual justice. Couple this with the inherent distrust of the state found within radical communities, and the fact that patriarchal socialization leaves even the most ardent anarchist susceptible to unconscious proliferation of abusive behavior, and what you've got is a space that needs to be filled, and SNY stepped in to do that.

At the time that my terrible behavior with Christina began, I was in the midst of helping facilitate three concurrent accountability processes with three different abusive men. I certainly felt a sense of disgust with myself, chastising these people for behaviors I was participating in, but I also let my participation in forms of feminist activism in other parts of my life obscure the harm I was causing to my partner. How did I get away with this? By being slightly drunk all the time and pretending that I was passively swayed by uncontrollable outside forces rather than being an active participant in making decisions that had outcomes and impacts in my life and the lives of those around me.

Just to really bring this point home: this stuff was All My Fault. I was behaving like a manipulative piece of shit, even if

I pretended I was just "doing what I had to do." But Slice Harvester was going well, at least. Somehow, through it all, I never faltered in my obligation to pizza reviewing. In fact, my writing became the one part of my life that wasn't stressful. It was an escape from the persistent, nagging fears of my day-to-day, and a chance for me to have unself-conscious fun, to be playful. As I continued to make my way through Midtown, eating unexceptional slices and finding clever ways to describe how gross or boring they were, the crummy pizza didn't even sadden me anymore. I knew I would make it downtown one day, and that somewhere below Fourteenth Street there was a perfect slice of pizza waiting for me.

During this time I did some really fun pizza eating, too. I went Slice Harvesting in Times Square with local folk musician and comic-book artist Jeffrey Lewis, who finally convinced me to institute a uniform rating system for all my reviews. Characteristically, I decided on a totally counterintuitive system. All pizzerias would receive a rating between zero and eight slices, with zero slices being the absolute worst a slice could possibly get, four being totally average, and eight being utter perfection. Had my rating system been in place for my previous reviews, for instance, Hell's Kitchen Pizza would have received a half slice because it was so gross I barfed it up, The World Famous Little Italy would've received a four because it's inoffensively average, and Gino's would've received a seven for being nearly perfect.

I also went out on a Slice Harvest with the band Hot New Mexicans, five touring punks from Athens, Georgia. On that particular day I was joined by my kid sister and my old friends Ella and Kevers as well—nine people in all, including me. I learned that there *is* such a thing as too many people on a pizza mission. We stood out far more in the pizza places because we were such a large group, it was difficult to take notes because there was always more than one person talking at a time, and our whole day was derailed for about forty-five minutes because one of the Georgians got lost in the subway. Oy yoy yoy. At least I learned a valuable lesson.

At one point I didn't update my blog for, like, two weeks or something, because Tina and I went to Miami so I could meet her mom. During that time I got an e-mail from this dude Thomas, a frequent commenter on my blog, that said, "Hey, where you been? I hope you're okay." I told him I was and thanked him for caring. He wrote back:

> Not just me, Bro. Last year I was on a plane from Singapore to NY—I started talking to this guy working in the backwaters of Malaysia. He was visiting NY for the first time and looking forward to getting pizza.
>
> I asked him if he needed recommendations. He said no, he knew where to go because he'd been reading this blog from some guy who was eating at every pizza place—your blog.

Think about that! Some dude in Malaysia was reading my blog. I know that's probably normal for all these Tumblr teens, but for me, a humble suburban punk rocker living out my dreams in the Big City, that was just mind-blowing.

And listen, things with Tina weren't all bad. It might seem

that way, but, like, I did all this crummy stuff and she didn't dump me. She stuck around for a reason. Maybe we each thought the other was an ultimate babe. Maybe we had mutually compatible pheromones. Maybe we had both just been looking for someone to spend time with who wanted to wear weird wigs and lip-sync to Abba songs. Who knows? Whatever the reason, we built a real love on that rickety foundation. I'm talkin' 'bout a *real love*—someone to set my heart free.

The reason I'm telling you this is because, while that stuff is cool, it's not very exciting. So where's the drama, you might be wondering. Where's the excitement at this point in our story? It's certainly not in the moments of pure, sweet joy. It's not in the synchronicity of our personalities, nor in the electricity of our touch. It's not in the late-night bus and bike rides to see each other, nor in the moments stolen from sleep. It's definitely not in how well we danced together or how it felt when we kissed.

That's not the stuff you want to hear. You want to hear about me making her cry, over the phone, on her birthday. You want to hear about her throwing a steel-toed boot through my window, toppling my bookshelves like some two-bit thug from a Walter Moseley novel one day while we were screaming at each other. You want to hear about the time she threatened to leave and I freaked out and cried and stomped and shouted and started tattooing her name on my arm with India ink and a sewing needle duct taped to a pen I stole from the bank. She made me stop because it was clearly off-center, and eventually we were both on the floor laughing. You can still see the faint *C* on my right wrist, like a war memorial.

The night Tina found out I was working at the bar, she didn't believe me at first. See, what happened was, it was a slow night. By two a.m., there was just one lady in there drinking. At one point the two of us went out front for a cigarette. Normally I would smoke in the back, but since I was working alone I had to go out front so that if a new customer showed up, I could get back behind the bar. You get it.

Anyway, there I was, standing out on the street with my one customer, making some bullshit small talk. I was pretty drunk by this point in the night and was just kinda counting down the hours till I could go home and pass out. Imagine my surprise when all of a sudden an entire bicycle came flying across the sidewalk to hit the rollgate of the vegetable stand next to me. Imagine my further surprise when I noticed that it was the bike I had just built for Christina.

She was biking past on her way home from a friend's house when she saw me standing outside the bar talking to some lady. She knew I was supposed to be at work, and so she assumed, since I had lied to her about being at work, that I was secretly dating this other woman. Then she did what any sensible person would do when they saw their boyfriend on a date with someone else: she got off her bike, lifted it over her head, and threw it at me.

My customer quickly shuffled back into the bar. I tried to explain the situation—that I wasn't on a date, that I *was* at work, that I worked at the bar now and had been meaning to tell her but it kept slipping my mind, and this was for the best and I was making more money and I didn't have to work outside anymore and another excuse, and another explanation, and it goes on and on forever.

She was mad that I lied to her. That's reasonable. You find out your alcoholic boyfriend has been secretly working at a bar, maybe you get a little mad. I was really drunk, though, and I wanted her to just "be cool," which I think basically means "don't have any opinions and be okay with me doing whatever I want." And when she wouldn't "be cool," *I* got mad. Much like the night she tried to talk to me about my drinking being problematic, I felt uncomfortable and so I lashed out. "You think just because we're dating you get to police everything I do? I don't go around telling you how to live YOUR fucking LIFE, so don't you DARE tell me how to live mine. Working at the bar makes sense, it's the right thing, it's good for me, and if you don't like it, you can fuck off." So she did. She flipped me the bird, got on her bike, and rode away. I went back into the bar and got incredibly wasted. My one customer left at three, and it didn't look like anyone else was coming in, so I locked the door an hour early and drank all the whiskey in the universe.

Some time around five thirty or six, I suspect, I let myself out of the bar and headed home, though I don't remember locking up or leaving or walking the few blocks to my house. I just know that at seven that morning I woke up slumped against my apartment door with my keys in my hand. My next-door neighbor's door was open and her kids, who must have been on their way to school, were staring at me wide-eyed. She lifted her children over my prone body one at a time, gave me an admonishing glare, and headed down the stairs. I let myself into my apartment and passed out on my kitchen floor for the next ten or so hours.

I woke up to about ninety million missed calls and text messages. They started out in basic "WHAT IS YOUR FUCKING PROBLEM" territory, but they eventually made their way into the "hi are you alive? are you okay???" zone. I wiped the dirt off my cheek, rolled a cigarette, and braced myself to call Christina.

The phone rang. She answered but said nothing.

"Hi. Hey, listen, I'm alive. Sorry. I got really drunk after we fought."

". . ."

"I know you're mad. You have every right to be mad. I'm sorry I got mad back. That was stupid."

". . ."

"I was drunk. I know that's a problem. I'll stop drinking at work, but really, this job is so much better than working delivery. I understand if you're uncomfortable, but hopefully we can talk about it."

". . ."

"I just . . . What are you thinking? I'd like to have a conversation about this. I'm really sorry."

". . ."

"How are we supposed to talk about this if you won't talk? Just tell me what you're thinking. Please."

". . ."

"PLEASE!"

She took a deep breath. "YOU WANNA KNOW WHAT I'M THINKING? I'M THINKING YOU'RE A FUCKING ASSHOLE LIAR IS WHAT I'M THINKING. WHAT ELSE ARE YOU LYING ABOUT?"

And she hung up.

I started to consider that maybe I should stop drinking for good.

CHAPTER 9

Amadeus Pizzeria

This slice was so soggy that when I folded it over it did that thing where it looks half like a neck bandana and half like a butthole. It tasted like a butthole, too. Just don't go here.

—*Slice Harvester Quarterly*, Issue 5, "Twenty-Third to Forty-Second Streets," visited on July 17, 2010

Opposite page: The labyrinth

Around this time I found myself listening to "Two-Way Street" by Slick Rick every morning. On the hook, he raps, "If goodness is what you're filling your soul with and you're looking for a woman you can chill and grow old with, who keeps no secrets (like who she creeps with): realize early it's a two-way street, kid." Now, Ricky the Ruler might not be the most sterling example of antipatriarchal thinking, but in this instance, he nailed it. If you're not being honest and up-front with your partner, how can you expect your partner to be open and honest with you? I knew I needed to get my shit together. Not just for Tina, but for myself.

I still didn't quit drinking altogether, but I signed up for a moderation management website, and every night I would log in and chart how many drinks I'd had on a spreadsheet. If I hadn't had any, that day's number appeared in an inspiring green; if I had between one and four drinks (ostensibly no more than one per hour), the number was a forgiving blue; and if I had more than four, the number glared a reproachful red.

I didn't like to see the red, so I used tricks: I'd take a Percocet or Klonopin to slightly augment the drinks I was having. Or I'd go to the bar at two thirty in the morning and have all four of my drinks in an hour and a half. It was still only four drinks that day! One night I got to the bar just in time to see a drinking buddy, Josh, show up. It was sometime around two. He had a job as a cook and had been at work all night, whereas I had been pacing my apartment staring at my watch since ten p.m., waiting until it was late enough to justify going to the bar.

We hugged and sat down at the bar together. I bought a round, he bought a round, I bought a round, he bought a round. As I was buying the fifth, I unconsciously muttered "Red five" under my breath.

"What the hell does that mean?" he asked me.

"What the hell does what mean?"

"Red five."

I hadn't realized I'd spoken out loud, and I was a little surprised. "Oh, it's nothing—it's just this dumb moderation thing I'm doing where I log how many drinks I have on a website, and if it's more than four, the number comes up red. It's so arbitrary." I was getting myself worked up. "I mean, who has only four drinks?"

He was appalled. "Four drinks?! What if you go to a barbecue?"

"What if I go to a show?"

"What if you go on a date?"

"What if I'm out dancing?"

"What if you had a hard day at work?"

I paused compassionately. "Did *you* have a hard day at work?"

"Sure did."

"Wanna do a shot?"

"Sure do."

So I ordered us some nice whiskey. We touched our glasses,

drank our liquor, and leaned back in our chairs, satisfied. Neither of us spoke for a few minutes.

"You know," he interjected into the silence before pausing to sip his beer ruminatively, "it's kinda bullshit that neither one of us can imagine going out and having fun without having more than four drinks."

"I know." I had been thinking the same thing, but when Josh said it, I knew it was true. I thought about going home. I mean, I liked Josh—we had good conversational chemistry, and he liked to drink, but we'd already been hanging out for an hour or so; wasn't that enough? I could go home right then if I wanted to, but what was I gonna do there—look at the internet? At least here I was interacting with a human being who was right in front of my face. "I mean, I know it's bullshit or whatever, but you wanna do another shot?"

He nodded his head yes.

A few weeks later on a hot July afternoon, 220 slices since Slice Harvester began, I met my friends Eliza and BBC (which stands for Big Brother Chris) to eat pizza. Of the two, I had gotten to know Eliza first. We'd been drunk and done drugs together at parties and shows, definitely had some wild times and shared some best friends, but at some point we were both trying to help our respective BFFs kick dope and would hang out at the falafel place she was working at and kvetch to each other, because we didn't want to put too much pressure on our friends but we needed an outlet to process all those *feelings* that come with someone you love and care about lying to you all the time. I don't need you to point out the irony. I'm right there with you.

But it wasn't all grim. Eliza and I ate a lot of pizza and Chinese food together. In fact, the first time I met BBC for real was when I tagged along for a slice with him and Eliza. He's maybe a year or two older than me, but he definitely had that "cool senior" vibe, along with the greasiest hair I had ever seen. I've always been intensely drawn to older boys with long, greasy hair. I don't know why, but tall, dark, mysterious greaseballs have always seemed like the gatekeepers to everything awesome. It probably all goes back to Jordan Catalano. Jared Leto turning out to be a weird Dad Rocker and not the ultimate Mainstream Outsider Cool Guy is basically my generation's 9/11.

Whatever; greasy weirdos are great in general, but BBC in particular is *incredible*. BBC fact list: he went to every punk show and just, like, lurked around looking so cool but not really talking to anyone; he sang in a band called Tender Wizards (RIGHT?!) who kind of sounded like the Peechees—guitar overdriven till the separate chords were barely discernible insistent drums, a loping bass line holding it all together, and on top of it all, BBC's strident screams about god only knows what; he lived at the punk house but secretly also had an apartment upstate because he had a job there as a physicist helping to build a particle collider. That last one is still so unbelievable to me. Greaseball Rock'n'Roll Physicist is the new Hot American Dude archetype. Y'all can have that one for free.

The day we went to eat pizza was a red-number morning, but I had been out with Eliza and BBC the night before, so at least we were all experiencing the dreary stages of a hangover. As some form of cosmic punishment for not adhering to my moderation routine, it ended up taking us almost two hours to get to Midtown from my Williamsburg apartment, a trip that normally took a trim twenty-five minutes. Over the course of those hours, walking between stations, sitting on trains that stalled out in tunnels, waiting on sweaty platforms, we all developed monstrous appetites. But when we finally got above ground and saw our first destination, right outside the subway station, we were decidedly *not* excited.

The place was called Pizza Suprema (generic Italian-sounding name), and it had a giant banner hanging above the entrance:

Awarded
"One of the 10
BEST PIZZAS IN N.Y.C."

And when I say giant, I'm talking six feet tall and, like, thirty feet wide. It covered up two windows of the apartment above the pizzeria. It was positively ostentatious. And it also seemed too ambivalent a boast to warrant such a huge sign. Like, who awarded that? Had they eaten at every pizzeria? The whole thing just rubbed me the wrong way.

We walked inside, and it looked like any run-of-the-mill pizza parlor. There were a ton of people, but it was lunchtime, and we were a few blocks from Port Authority, right across the street from Penn Station, so the crowd didn't seem exceptional in the least. I ordered our slice from the guy, and he grabbed a piece of pizza from a pie sitting under the Plexiglas, plopped it on a tray, and slid it over to me.

We trudged to our table, expecting nothing special. I took my first bite and passed the slice to Eliza, who took a bite and passed it over to BBC. By the time it got back to me, we had all chewed and swallowed our first taste and were looking at each other, jaws agape. This was the best pizza I had eaten in years. I took another bite without saying anything and passed it on. We ate the whole slice in astonished silence. When we finished, a quick consensus was reached, and we ordered another. At this point in Slice Harvesting, I had eaten at over two hundred different pizzerias, and I had *never* gotten a second slice. I had come close at a couple of places, but it never seemed worth it to jeopardize my appetite. Pizza Suprema was the exception.

The slice was everything I ever wanted. The dough was thin and crisp, perfectly salted, and crunched when it folded. The sauce and cheese created a delicious flavor combination and melded in perfect quantities. And there was that special something—that New York magic that makes a Ramones song timeless and a Screeching Weasel song boring. It is impossible to characterize in words—a mystical, modern-day witchery.

Feelings that are similar to eating magic pizza: when music perfectly matches the weather or your mood (Billie Holiday on a trembly tape deck when it's rainy; Cam'ron out a car window at the beginning of summer, drinking a beer on the stoop with your pals with Thee Headcoatees on the jambox, Lee Moses on spring evenings, etc.); the sense of relief and/or exultation felt when you've been having an ambiguous "not a date but not *not* a date" hangout with someone you've been crushing on and tension has been mounting all day, and then you finally hold hands or have some other affirmation that The Feeling Is Mutual; finding a rare record or book or stamp or baseball card or shirt or coin or whatever the fuck you collect in a thrift store or at a garage sale or whatever; when you look so sharp right after a haircut and you got on your new black jeans that fit just right and you know you're going to be the flyest person in whatever space you'll be in for at least the next couple of hours, if not the next few days. What these disparate moments share is the feeling of everything falling into place, the feeling that regardless of all the external bummers of day-to-day living, things are at least momentarily going your way; the fates are smiling down on you. Maybe your feelings aren't the same as mine; maybe for you eating a perfect slice feels like stealing home in your softball league, your kid getting straight As, or slam-dunking the Henderson account. You get the point, though. The right slice makes it all feel okay.

Eliza, BBC, and I didn't have another transcendent slice after Suprema. In fact, the slice directly across the street at Amadeus Pizzeria was especially horrid. But the day certainly stayed interesting. We ate at a couple of crap places, totally unexceptional slices. Nothing worth mentioning until we gooned our way into the underground shopping mall that sits below Penn Station. There's something very sci-fi about being in this literally subterranean place of commerce. I've always liked places of transience—train stations, bus depots, rest stops, on-ramps, freight yards—places where it feels like, if I were desperate or courageous enough, I could start my life all over again from scratch somewhere else, simply by boarding whatever means of conveyance was at hand.

Sometimes when I'm feeling crunchy I think that maybe when I'm in those transient places I'm especially in tune with the universe, that I can feel things that not everyone else feels, that I can pick up an extrasensory wavelength that only certain people are privy to. In these locales, these Between Places, I feel comfort and peace in the lack of stability. So much frenetic energy buzzing all around, and here I am, stationary, watching. I could leave, too, if I so desired—just walk up to a window and buy a ticket to somewhere. Travel imbues everyone and everything with a sense of vast potential. Everyone could be anyone. Everything could be anything.

So it is at Penn Station. And inside Penn Station is a sprawling mall. There are nearly a hundred shops and restaurants, four banks, and access to six different transportation services that could ultimately ferry you to anywhere in the US or Canada. I don't think anyone actually comes inside Penn Station specifically to eat or shop; I think the incidental traffic of the three hundred thousand people who pass through there on any given day is enough to sustain so many businesses. This makes for an interesting dynamic. Since no particular place is anything more than an impulsive destination for the various comers and goers, even amid the chaos of commuters there's a feeling of being on a slow, casual stroll. "Should we eat at Columbo Yogurt or Zaro's Bread Basket? Maybe we'll just grab something quick from Planet Smoothie and have a real meal when we get where we're going." So many options! But eating in Penn Station is also a game of chance. The place is labyrinthine and huge. What will you be offered in the course of your walk from the entrance to your platform? Dare you risk missing your train and venture out of the way to find something better? Every trip through Penn Station is a throw of the dice.

My friends and I, however, had a destination: Don Pepe Pizza, which was everything I could've wanted a pizzeria inside a science-fiction mall to be: neon lights everywhere, and some of the most bizarre humans I've ever seen camped out at the tables seemingly since before time began. One dude, an older gentleman with unintentional dreadlocks wearing white velour pants, a white down coat, white Timberlands, and a white knit cap (though all of his gear had taken on the same pervasive grayish-brown hue that my white T-shirts had, a patina the Punx lovingly refer to as "permadirt"), looked like an urban yeti. He had various dusty tomes spread out before him—multiple volumes of an encyclopedia, an art book, some sheaves of photocopied paper—and was taking notes in what looked like the Enochian alphabet. And the pizza was good to boot! It had nothing on Suprema—the ratios were a bit off—but overall, the ingredients were decent, the slice was warm and enjoyable, and, most important, it satisfied us.

There is something very special about Don Pepe Pizza. It's a place I feel should exist only in my dreams or in the dystopian future presented in a William Gibson or Neal Stephenson novel. But it is real, one of the many unsung wonders of New York City. Step right up to the sci-fi pizzeria! Marvel at the Urban Yeti and his mysterious, hermetic alphabet! Witness the Slice Harvester defy the laws of god and man by eating his tenth consecutive slice of pizza! Smell the odor produced by three hundred thousand commuters! See the Adult Frat Babies, the Modern-Day Sweathogs, the whole rowdy gang! Enter if you thirst for adventure, but enter at your own risk!

By Halloween, Tina and I had patched things up a bit, and she took a trip to visit the Good Witch of Philadelphia for a weekend. I took the train into the city and waited around with her for the bus, like a good boyfriend does. After watching her depart, I wondered what to do with myself, and then I realized I was only a few blocks from Pizza Suprema. I decided to head back there to see if the slice was as good as I remembered.

When I got there, I noticed that they had blown up my review into a huge poster and plastered it in the front window, facing the street. This was the first time, as far as I knew, that a pizza place had publicly acknowledged my work. I walked in, wondering whether they'd spot me. The place was bustling, and there was a guy behind the counter who was clearly the owner. I approached him and asked, "You own this place?"

He looked me over. "Yeah, why?"

"Well, I wrote the review that you have blown up in the window."

He literally dropped the soda he was holding, sprinted out from behind the counter, and lifted me up in a bear hug. After a second he realized that it was maybe not polite to lift a grown man whom he didn't even know off the ground. He set me down gently and put out his hand to shake. "I'm Joe. This was my father's place. I knew you'd come back."

And that was how our friendship began. During the course of it, over dozens of Suprema slices, he told me the story you're about to read.

CHAPTER 10

Pizza Suprema

Even straight out of the oven, the slice at Suprema had that crisp crunch one expects from a good slice. The ratios on this slice were superb; there was ample grease, and the whole thing was moist without being sloppy. The sauce, which BBC thought *might* be the best part (though none of us could agree on a *best* part of this delectable slice), was integrated very nicely with the cheese (which was absolutely delish), so that they were discernible from each other in flavor but still totally enmeshed, creating a wonderful texture atop the crispness of the crust. And the crust's flavor was unstoppable!

—*Slice Harvester Quarterly*, Issue 5, "Twenty-Third to Forty-Second Streets," visited on July 17, 2010

Opposite page: A young Sal Riggio

In April 1937, Maria Riggio—wife to Giuseppe Riggio, mother to Jovanna, Lucia, Rosalita, and Vita Riggio—realized she was pregnant for the fifth time. The baby was conceived before her husband had returned to America, where he was attempting to build the family fortune in the coal mines of Illinois. He had left Maria and the four girls in Burgio, the provincial Sicilian *comune*, or village, where they had lived their whole lives. Burgio, with a current population of a little over three thousand (smaller than the student body at my suburban high school), was only slightly larger in the thirties. We're talking about a tiny town, in a rural province. I imagine it was a lot like Fellini's *Amarcord*—beautiful scenery, cool ancient buildings, dusty streets, and everyone's a pervert. Well, maybe not that last part.

Maria's brothers, who worked her husband's land for her, were stealing her money, leaving her with barely enough to feed herself and her four daughters. For her fifth pregnancy, she desperately wanted a son. She had been hoping for a son during all her pregnancies, but her body seemed to create only more women. Blame the patriarchal culture she was immersed in, but this was a problem for her.

Maria went to see her aunt Cecilia, who was a sort of provincial Catholic mystic. She explained her problem—that she needed a son to carry on the family name, and was scared she would have another daughter. Her elderly aunt put a comforting, wrinkled hand on her shoulder. "Don't worry, child. All will be well. Trust in God."

Maria came home from seeing Cecilia, lit a candle, said her prayers, and went to bed. That night she had a vivid dream. She saw her father-in-law, Salvatore Riggio, standing in the center of a large hall, surrounded by the entire family. In front of him was an enormous round loaf of bread. In one hand he held a knife, which he used to cut the loaf into triangular wedges. He distributed these wedges one at a time to everyone in the family. When he handed Maria her piece, she woke up in a sweat, but she knew everything would be okay. She would have a boy, and he would bring abundance and prosperity to the family.

Sal Riggio, named for his paternal grandfather, was born seven months later, on the twenty-seventh of November. Though his memories of his youth in Italy were of scarcity and hunger, he always seemed preternaturally lucky. His family likes to say there was an angel looking over his shoulder. Once when he was five, little Sal went out to a field with some older boys to play. They played a children's gambling game, in which kids would stand coins upright like dominoes in the dirt and take turns throwing pebbles at them. Whatever coins the player toppled were his to keep. Sal had never played the game before and seemed like an easy mark for the older kids, but he proved to have an aptitude for it. After a few rounds, he had won half of the other kids' money.

Although he was only five, Sal realized quickly that these kids were going to kick his ass if he kept taking their money, so he devised a plan: he would lose on purpose until he was left with the money he'd started out with, and then he would go home. The problem was, no matter how hard he tried to sabotage himself, no matter how badly he threw his pebble, he couldn't seem to lose. Things were getting tense. Sal didn't know what to do, but he kept trying to miss. And then, just as he had taken almost all of the other guys' coins, as tensions were boiling and a beating was imminent, he heard his mother calling him home for dinner. Sal tossed a handful of his winnings on the ground as a peacemaking gesture and ran home, narrowly escaping calamity. He didn't get his ass beaten, but those kids never played with him again.

When he was nine, Sal's family made their way across the Atlantic to America, where he met his father for the first time. Giuseppe had left the coal mines and relocated to Bushwick, Brooklyn, and rented a modest apartment at 76 George Street, where Sal spent most of his childhood. The apartment wasn't big enough for the whole family, but Sal's sisters got married one by one and moved out.

Bushwick in the forties was a changing neighborhood. "The Germans moved out when the Italians moved in," Joe told me with a laugh during one of our many conversations about his father's life. Giuseppe took a job in Brooklyn as a box burner, which was actually a job back in the day. Think about that for a second. Think about how different society was less than a hundred years ago. Burning boxes was unskilled labor; it was toxic and exhausting and didn't pay well, but Giuseppe had saved up some coal mining money, and working as a box burner was enough to get by.

Sal's whole family was "in pizza." It started with Sal's eldest brother-in-law, Pino, married to Sal's sister Jovanna, who opened up J & V Pizza on Eighteenth Avenue in Bensonhurst in 1950 with Rosalia's husband, Vinny, who still owns the place. In fact, the other night Aaron Cometbus and I took the N train out to Eighteenth Avenue at around eleven p.m. to check out the place, and let me tell you, the pizza is not the best I've ever had, but the store is a Dream Come True—totally dark and cavernous, with a couple of boisterous, half-friendly/half-terrifying pizza men and a TV playing some unrecognizable old movie on cable. As Aaron and I ate our slices, I noticed an older white woman in a sundress with her hair shellacked into some sort of peculiar helmet and straight-up black circles around her eyes as though she were a raccoon in a kabuki theater. She was watching the television intently, slowly sipping a can of cola through a straw.

She slurped her last sip of soda and began to collect her many bags just as Aaron and I were finishing our pizza. I thought maybe this lady was a longtime regular and could give me a rundown on how things had been Back In The Day, so I turned to her as she passed our table and asked, "You been coming here a while?" as casually as I could.

She blinked her eyes twice and stared at me for a few seconds before she began to speak in the most adorable outer-borough falsetto I have ever heard. "Oh yeaaah, ya know, I like ta come heeah en eat aliddle pizza, trink a soda, en wash the tel-o-vision. Today I only got a soda, though, becaurse I went ta da theata an it costa lotta money fah theata tickets, so I only got a soda. Now I wanna use tha bah-troom, but the man is mopping and he won't let me." Then she blinked a few more times and walked off into the night.

But anyway, back to 1950. Sal's brother-in-law Pino lived across the street from a pizza shop in Bushwick that did a pretty good business, and he wanted in. So he called Vinny, because, as Joe puts it, "Vinny, being Neapolitan, knew something about pizza," and they opened up J & V. Family legend has it that Pino was the first guy in America to shred the mozzarella instead of just laying it on the pie in slabs.

But Sal wasn't necessarily interested in the family business. He was a smart and bookish kid who excelled at school, a model student at Bushwick High with aspirations of becoming a doctor. He worked summers at J & V, where he learned to make pizza, but he didn't want to work with his hands like his father had.

In 1954, when Sal was seventeen, Pino and Vinny's partnership was on the rocks, and Sal's father offered to buy him Pino's half of the business. Sal refused. He wanted more for himself than to sweat his life away in a hot pizzeria. That same year, Pino's daughter, Rose, who was Sal's age, and her older husband, Tony, opened up Valenti's Pizza on Fifth Avenue in the Italian enclave of Park Slope. Everyone around Sal was getting into pizza, but Sal had no interest.

Straight out of high school, Sal took a job for Western Union as a messenger. He loved learning the streets of New York so intimately, but it was grueling work that sometimes required him to go to dangerous neighborhoods. The place he hated most in the whole city was the Main Post Office, at Thirty-First Street and Eighth Avenue. The neighborhood was filthy and decrepit, teeming with violence, seemingly forgotten by City Hall. Sal swore to himself that whatever he did next, he would spend as little time as possible in that urban hell.

By the end of his first month as a messenger he had worn holes in the bottoms of his shoes, and had to spend an entire week's pay on a new pair. He resolved to work his way up the chain at Western Union, and was eventually promoted to the position of dispatcher, where he worked in an office and wore a collared shirt. But the pay was just as lousy, even though the job sounded more prestigious. Like Joe told me, "They may give you bigger titles, but they don't give you bigger paychecks."

By 1960 Vinny had paid off the loans he'd taken out to open J & V, and the shop was starting to turn a pretty substantial profit. Vinny had never had money before, but once he did, he knew what to do with it. He bought a house, nice clothes, a new car every year. He bought his wife jewelry. He sent his kids to military school. Sal looked at himself, slaving away at Western Union for a pittance, and looked at Vinny, who seemed to have it all. Sure, he had spent years drenched in sweat, slinging pizza from morning till night, but he had something to show for it. What did Sal have? A fancy-sounding title and no money.

So he opened up his first pizza shop, Elegante Pizza, on Fifth Avenue in Bay Ridge. Sal's partner in the business—we'll call him Tony Bologna—was a shifty layabout who spent more time flirting with the female customers than doing actual work. In 1963, Sal went back to Burgio for six months to meet Maria, his soon-to-be bride in what was essentially an arranged marriage between family friends. He left Tony in charge of Elegante, knowing full well the place might not even be open anymore when he got back.

The way the Riggio family tells it, and I have no idea whether this bears out historical fact, in the sixties, pizza was a regional food in Naples, but hadn't spread all over Italy. It was images of teens slamming slices on Friday night in American pop culture that popularized pizza throughout the rest of Italy and the rest of the world. To illustrate this fact, they cite a conversation between Sal and Maria's grandmother, also named Maria.

Grandma Maria cornered Sal in the kitchen of the family home, pointing an imposing, gnarled, girlfriend's grandmother's finger into his face. "How do you plan to support my granddaughter? What do you do? Why should we let you take her away to America?"

"I run a pizza parlor," he responded nervously.

"Pizza parlor? What's this?"

"I make and sell pizza."

"I don't understand; what is this stuff? What do you actually do?"

"PIZZA!" He was starting to get frustrated. "It's a food from Naples. I make dough, I roll it out flat, I put sauce and cheese on it, and I cook it in the oven."

Grandma Maria laughed a mean-spirited laugh. "That's how you're going to make a living to support my granddaughter? Okay, Mr. Baker. Good luck."

Six months later, Sal and Maria returned to America and found Elegante in shambles. Tony Bologna swore up and down to Sal that the pizza shop hadn't turned a profit the whole time he'd been gone. Rather than fight Mr. Bologna for his fair share of an already failing business, Sal sold Tony his half, and he and Maria opened up a new shop on Myrtle Avenue in Fort Greene. This proved to be a bad idea.

By the mid-sixties, Fort Greene had gone from a thriving working-class enclave to a grim, blighted wasteland. The Navy Yard had been decommissioned, and the Fort Greene Houses, which had previously housed Yard workers, had fallen into such disarray that they were described by *Newsweek* as "one of the starkest examples of the failure of public housing." They were characterized by "windows broken . . . walls cracking; light fixtures inoperable; doors unhinged; elevators that are clearly used as toilets."*

So, Myrtle Avenue in the mid-sixties was not a hospitable place for a pizza parlor. Rather than stick around the neighborhood and try to build connections to a community that clearly didn't want them there, Sal and Maria set their sights elsewhere. They knew they wanted to open a shop in Manhattan, but they weren't sure exactly where. They began to spend each day driving around the city in Sal's old Dodge Rambler, scoping out FOR RENT signs in windows. This was before Craigslist.

They drove all over the city, to no avail. One day about two weeks into their quest, Sal and Maria were pointed to a luncheonette at 413 Eighth Avenue, just south of Thirty-First

---

*The *Newsweek* article is quoted on page 169 of *An Architectural Guidebook to Brooklyn* by Francis Morrone. The Morrone text lacks a citation, and I have no idea how to find a *Newsweek* article from 1959.

Street, whose owners were looking to sell their lease. The space had a great interior, but the location was a nightmare for Sal. It was less than half a block from the Main Post Office he had spent so much time at as a messenger, in the neighborhood he hated more than any other, the neighborhood he swore he would avoid at all costs. Sal refused the space, though Maria had a good feeling about it.

For five more months, Sal and Maria drove around Manhattan. They widened their search to Brooklyn, but still came up empty. Every few weeks they would find themselves passing 413 Eighth Avenue, the FOR RENT sign still in the window. Maria would say, "Let's make them an offer." But every time Sal would decline.

After another month of nothing, they basically just said "Fuck it" and took the spot on Eighth. It was provisional; it was temporary. Sal knew how to open a pizza place, and he knew he wouldn't have to stay in this most-hated locale for very long if he didn't want to, but he knew he had to go somewhere. He wanted to start a family with Maria, and he couldn't do that in good conscience without a solid source of income.

Sal had used the money from selling his half of Elegante to buy a house on Sixteenth Avenue in Bensonhurst, so there was a home in which the family could begin, and now, with the lease for the storefront signed and filed, he had a business. The build-out was easy: they kept the floor from the luncheonette (it's still there today), installed a few banquettes, and put in a pizza oven and a counter. He didn't even bother to name the place—he just put up a big sign that said PIZZA, and that was that. Sal's nameless pizza parlor was open by the summer of 1964. Soon after,

Maria was pregnant. What perfect timing! The following spring, Maria gave birth to Mariella, their first daughter.

Business was slow at first, but it was enough for Sal to support his family and to fly his mother to the States to live in the house with them. He was the son, after all. It was his responsibility to care for her. And of course it didn't hurt that she could help with the child care.

Sal kept his costs low by providing as little as possible to his customers. He used misprinted boxes from other pizzerias, served his slices on pieces of wax paper instead of plates, and bought only unbleached paper bags, because it all saved a few cents. He never gave anybody a napkin unless they asked, and if they did ask, he would give napkins out one at a time. People would ask him for garlic powder, and he'd say, "No garlic"; they'd ask him why, and he'd say "'Cause it gives you agita." Maybe it gave him agita (which is Old People for heartburn), but that's not why Sal didn't have garlic powder. He didn't have it because he deemed it an unnecessary extravagance.

One place Sal never cut corners, however, was his pizza. He imported flour, tomatoes, and cheese from Italy, and he busted his ass to perfect his recipe. He only sold plain, round pies—no Sicilian, no white slices, no pepperonis or mushrooms. He only made plain pizza, and he worked tirelessly, constantly tweaking the ingredients to improve his pies.

In 1967, Sal's mother passed away. Two months later, the RCA Technical School opened up around the corner on Thirty-First Street, and Sal's pizza place became a popular hangout spot for blue-collar students looking for affordable meals. The sudden boom in business seemed like a parting gift from Maria Riggio.

In 1968, construction of Madison Square Garden was completed across Eighth Avenue, and though the main entrance to the Garden is on Seventh Avenue, that back-door traffic, combined with the steady trickle of RCA students, was more than enough to sustain a pizza place.

In 1969, Sal and Maria's son, Joe, was born. In 1972, their second daughter, Joanne, was born, and the Riggio family moved two blocks down to Fifteenth Avenue in Bensonhurst, where they bought a house across the street from Sal's sister Rosalie. It was definitely a nicer house, but in order to maintain the middle-class life Sal wanted for his family, he worked twelve hours a day, six days a week. In order to ensure that his kids would not suffer the spare, hungry childhood he had, Sal basically had to sacrifice his relationship with them. He never taught his son how to ride a bike or throw a ball; he wasn't there when his daughters took their first steps or said their first words; but they had a roof over their heads, and they had food to eat. That was what mattered to Sal. He could give up his own life to pull his family out of the cycle of poverty. Maybe if *he* worked hard enough, they could at least have relationships with *their* children.

Nineteen seventy-two was also the year that Sal finally perfected his slice. Ten houses down and across the street from the Riggios, a guy named Tony Dara lived with his family. Tony owned an industrial bakery that supplied all of Brooklyn's public schools with bread. He and Sal became friends, and one day while he was in Hell's Kitchen, Tony stopped into Sal's place for a slice.

"It's pretty good," he said, "but the dough could use a little work. This sauce is unbelievable, though. You let me show you how to make the dough a little better and you'll have the perfect piece of pizza."

Sal was a proud man, for sure, but he wasn't an idiot. If a master baker wanted to help him tweak the dough, so be it. He and Tony went into the back, and Sal learned the Dara Family Secret Pizza Dough Recipe. And lo, on this day, Sal's slice was perfected.

Joe visited the pizzeria for the first time when he was four years old. His mother dressed him up in a brand new peacoat so he could look like hot shit going to work with his dad. Sal stepped into the back to go over some paperwork, and his employee, also named Sal (we'll call him Salvatore, though, so we don't get confused), asked little Joe if he wanted to learn how to make pizza.

Joe was thrilled, to the extent that a four-year-old can be, at the chance to learn his father's trade. But within minutes there was flour everywhere, and his brand-new peacoat was covered in a fine white dust, as if he'd been putting up drywall all day. He took one look at his sullied clothes and broke down into the most intense sadness he had yet felt in his short life. His father was not someone he knew. The fact that they were out together was a rare occurrence. They barely had a rapport because Sal worked so much, and whenever he was home, he was mostly a tired, grumpy disciplinarian. Joe got scared; his emotions swept over him like a great wave, and he began to cry uncontrollable, torrential tears.

Sal came running out of his office to find his son on the floor, covered in flour, weeping nonstop. He rushed to Joe's side and lifted him up, with no concern for the flour that now coated him as well. He looked at his son with kind eyes and asked, "Joe, what's wrong?"

Joe's tears began to abate. He wiped away some snot. "I got my new coat all dirty. I'm sorry, Daddy. Don't be mad."

Sal looked down at his son, read the fear of reprisal in his face, and just melted. "Mad, Joey? How could I be mad at you?"

"Because I did something bad! I got my new coat dirty!"

"Forget the coat. Flour comes off. Your mother will clean it when we get home. The important thing is that you're here with me now. Let's get back to making this pie." And they finished rolling out the dough. Sal put down the sauce, and he let little Joe sprinkle the cheese.

By the time he was ten, Joe had begun to work at the pizza place most days. "I liked the idea, initially," he told me. "I was wearing my little shorts, workin' in the pizza place. And my dad would always say, 'If they ask you for your working papers, you're just helpin' out,' which I was. That's what sons are supposed to do. In the old days in Sicily, the son would watch the sheep. My job was to watch the cash register. That was my sheep."

As a teenager, Joe was sent to military school, which was apparently the thing to do for upwardly mobile Italian families in South Brooklyn in the 1980s. You send the son to military school to teach him some discipline. Sal wanted more for Joe than he ever had. He didn't begrudge the fact that he was doing exactly what he swore he never would—sweating it out in a pizza place, laboring with his hands instead of his mind—because it provided the financial stability needed to give his children the foundation of education to escape the poverty cycle. The American Dream at work, right in front of our very eyes. Huzzah!

The problem was that Joe *liked* working in the pizzeria, he *liked* making pizza, and he had ideas about how the place should be run. For one thing, he thought that maybe they should give the place a name, and that maybe there should be a sign outside with the name on it. And then maybe they should print that name on the pizza boxes instead of using other people's boxes, so that when people got pizza from them they would know where it came from.

"We can't be 'That place behind MSG' forever, Dad. How are we gonna sustain a customer base if no one knows what the hell we're called?"

"What's this 'we,' Joey?" Sal responded. "There is no 'we' here. I do this so you don't have to. I make enough now to send you to a good school. You'll go to college. What more do you want from me?"

But Joe wanted lots more. He would go down to his uncle Vinny's place in Bensonhurst to work sometimes, or to his uncle Tony's pizza place on Long Island, and they were making pepperoni pizza and Sicilian slices. Joe would ask his dad, "Why don't you do something like that? It's what people want." But Sal wouldn't budge. He had his way, and it had worked well enough so far. Why change it?

In 1987, Joe graduated high school. He stayed in the city for college, commuted from Bensonhurst to NYU to study philosophy in preparation for law school, and continued to work shifts at the pizza place a few times a week. He told me that in his philosophy classes they "talked a lot about *loving humanity*. It's easy to love humanity, because humanity doesn't smell, and humanity's not taking a shit on your floor—it's an abstraction. I remember coming around here to work lunch and watching humanity trying to rip us off—you know, saying 'I gave you a twenty.' It was basically the raw end of humanity. I'd see a guy out here every day, and his scam was to fill up an empty vodka bottle with water and then bang into, like, a businessman, and the bottle would crack on the floor and he would scream at the guy. And the businessman would get scared and give him twenty dollars to calm him down. The guy would do this all day. So this was the humanity that I knew. This wasn't the humanity that the ivory-towered professor was talking about."

In '88, the economy was in the shitter, the city had declared bankruptcy, and no one had any work. Always on the lookout for a bargain, Sal decided to renovate while construction prices were low. Besides, the place needed a makeover. By the time they reopened, Joe had worn Sal down enough that he conceded on everything. He would give his place a name, and he would start serving slices with toppings. It took nearly twenty-five years for him to make a decision that most other pizzeria owners had made a decade prior; hey, progress.

As for the name, one day while they were renovating Sal was sitting in the car outside Meat Supreme in Bay Ridge, waiting for Maria to finish shopping. He looked up at the sign and thought, "Okay, that's a name." And there it was. He called a sign guy and had them make up a little number that said PIZZA SUPREME. However, some guy in Massapequa already had a place called Pizza Supreme, and he sent Sal a cease-and-desist letter from a lawyer. They changed the name to Suprema "because it sounded more Italian and was easier than dealing with litigation."

With all the renovations done, Pizza Suprema was really going. Everything was great: the neighborhood was getting a little safer, and Sal was loosening up the reins a bit, accepting some suggestions and criticisms. He started using plates. He bought some garlic powder. They still had to keep the oregano behind the counter to stop the drug dealers from stealing it and selling it as weed, there were still destitute old men in the process of drowning in booze passed out all over the place, but more and more people were coming to the Garden to watch sports or whatever, and the pizzeria was developing a name for itself, now that it had a name to develop.

Days passed; Sal worked. Years passed; Sal worked. One by one the kids grew up, got married, and moved out. Sal worked and worked. He never took a vacation. He'd been working his whole life. He wouldn't have known what to do with himself on vacation, and god forbid he should retire.

In 1996, Joe passed the bar and began practicing law. "My father was so proud of me," he told me, "but I was more proud of him. I thought what he did was more noble than what I did. I couldn't believe how litigious our society was. It was insane. Frivolous lawsuits were rampant, and it sucked to be a part of that system. And in a way, you can't do anything more noble than feed people. I wanted to do that, too. This might sound a little sentimental for a grown man, but I wanted to be like my dad. He never wanted me to take over this business, though. He didn't even want me to make pizza.

"I loved the business 'cause I grew up in it, but the way he saw it, it was demeaning manual labor. He had wanted to be a doctor or a lawyer, and he was prevented from following that dream because of his circumstances. He wanted what he thought was better for me. So I became a lawyer, even though I hated it."

In 1998, during my induction ceremony into the International Punk Gang on the tiny stage in the men's room at CBGB, I swore an oath of disloyalty to Rudy Giuliani by reciting the lyrics to "New York City Is Dead" by the LES Stitches (*You can't drink on the street or even take a leak / Now even forty-deuce is clean!*), and I still hold tight to a staunch anti-Giuliani ethos today. However, even I have to admit that though Rudy's policies were racist, classist, and borderline fascist, his authoritarian strategy was probably a boon for *some* of the small businesses in *some* of the neighborhoods his police invaded. Which is just to say, Pizza Suprema, through no fault of their own and no active participation in the machinations of City Hall, only did better as the city got "cleaned up" from the mid-nineties through the post-9/11s.

In 2007, Sal had a heart attack at work and was taken to the hospital, where he passed away during surgery. With Sal's death, a question arose: would Suprema continue? And how? Of the three kids, Joe was the only one who knew the pizza business. It took him no time to come to a decision. He quit the law firm and took over the pizza place. All told, Suprema was closed only on the day of the funeral.

It wasn't easy to step into Sal's shoes. Making pizza was easy; Joe had been doing it since he was a kid. But by 2007, a majority of the customers were regulars who had been coming in for years, some of them for their entire lives. They all wanted to know what happened to Sal, so Joe had to narrate the story of his father's death again and again and again. Other people simply thought the pizzeria had changed hands, and they didn't like that. The regular pizza eater, much like Sal Riggio, doesn't take well to change. When there's a new guy behind the counter at your pizza place, suddenly the pizza might seem a little different. And maybe it *is* different, but maybe it's just a reverse placebo effect: the visible human change creates the illusion of change in the pizza. People would say, "I don't know if I'm gonna come here anymore; the pizza changed," which made Joe furious.

Joe told me, "I'd say 'I've been working here since I was a kid.' And they didn't believe me, so I'd have to find a guy to say, 'I've been coming here for thirty years, and I remember when Joe couldn't reach the counter.'

"It was the Italians and the Greeks who gave me the most shit. They'd say it changed. How could it have changed? I've been making this dough since I was twelve years old. I started making pizza when I was thirteen. And all this new stuff? I fought for this stuff. For example, I brought stuffed pizza here. And now Pasqualle's complaining, 'The stuffed pizza's not as good. Your father used to make it better.' My father didn't even know what stuffed pizza was!"

But Joe persevered, and life moved on. He added fresh mozzarella slices to the menu, he added sausage rolls, he started buying fresh mushrooms instead of those nasty canned ones most pizza parlors use. Most important, he installed a half dozen napkin dispensers on the walls and put spice shakers out on each table. Give the people what they want.

In the autumn of 2009, the *New York Post* was getting ready to run an article about this kid named Sean Taylor, who spends every October eating only pizza. Sean had decided to feature Pizza Suprema as one of his favorite places, and Joe was looking forward to the press. He thought it was the beginning of something good. People would finally know about Suprema, about his dad's legacy.

But one day in September, Sean came into Suprema with bad news. "The *Post* cancelled the article. The *Daily News* just ran a piece about some guy who's gonna eat a slice at every pizza place in the city. The reporter says his editor told him we can't do my article anymore. They don't want to seem like they're copying." Sean was understandably crestfallen, and Joe commiserated with him, but as soon as Sean left, Joe walked to the deli next door and forked over fifty cents for a copy of the *Daily News*. He flipped to the third page, found the article about me, and knew I would pick Suprema.

So he followed the blog, watching my progress down the island of Manhattan. I don't know whether he was at the pizza shop the day Eliza and BBC and I came in. If he was, he certainly didn't recognize me. In fact, when I walked back in that day in October after taking Tina to Port Authority to catch her bus to Philly, I ordered my slice unnoticed. It was only when I saw Joe behind the counter and introduced myself that we became friends and he introduced me to his mom, and over the course of many months they told me the wonderful story I just told you.

You wanna hear something amazing? This one afternoon we were sitting in there, Joe and I, waiting for his mom to show up so I could interview her about Italy. By way of small talk, Joe said, "You grew up around the city, right? What was your favorite slice as a kid?"

My eyes immediately glazed over in trancelike reverie as I intoned, "St. Marks Pizza. It was this little place on Third Avenue just off St. Marks. Everyone who went there loved it, but I'm not sure it was such a big deal in the pizza world, and if you weren't hanging around the East Village in the nineties, you probably didn't get to go."

Joe smirked. "I think my neighbor owned that place. I'll be right back." He stepped outside to make a call. I bit my nails as I watched him through the window. When he hung up the phone and came back inside, he was beaming.

Guess who owned St. Marks Pizza! C'mon, it's not a guess if you just keep reading. Really, take a second and guess in your head. Okay, did you guess yet? I like making people guess stuff. Tina hates it. *Anyway*, you wanna know the answer? It was

Tony Dara. Tony fucking Dara, from ten houses down and across the street on Sixteenth Avenue in Bensonhurst. Tony Dara, who taught Sal Riggio how to make dough.

Listen to this shit: Tony Dara, if you recall, owned an industrial bakery that had contracts with a number of the elementary schools in South Brooklyn. Well, in the late eighties, the city defaulted on a bunch of payments to Tony's bakery, and he realized that city contracts were a fool's game. He sold off his warehouse and all his equipment and decided he wanted to go into business on a smaller scale, with a higher profit margin. An older guy in the neighborhood was moving back to Sicily and offered to sell Tony his pizza parlor in the East Village.

Tony agreed, and then immediately called up Sal Riggio. He said, "Sal, listen, I just bought this pizza place. Can you do me a solid and teach me how to make your sauce? Also, what cheese do I gotta buy? I got the dough down, but I need your help with the rest of this."

And Sal was all, "A'ight, fam," and taught him how to make pizza.

Do you understand what this means? This means that my original favorite slice of pizza, a slice that I ate for the first time when I was thirteen, from a place that shut down in 2003, and to which I probably stopped going regularly in 2001, used the same recipe as the only place to which I gave a perfect slice review out of the almost four hundred different pizza places in Manhattan. You may not agree with my taste in pizza, but you at least have to admit that I'm consistent. Of course, I wouldn't learn of the Suprema–St. Marks connection until long after I had finished Harvesting, and I still had plenty of Manhattan to cover—and another Blast from the Past was waiting for me, though this one would prove to be unpleasant.

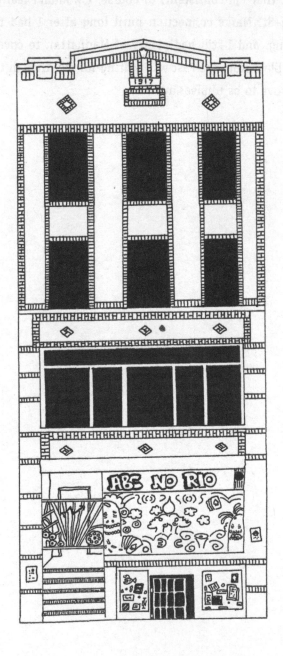

CHAPTER 11

Nonna's

A few bites in, the crust just ruptured and split. It looked like when there's an earthquake in *He-Man* or that awesome old X-Men cartoon and the ground splits apart in jagged chunks and there are swirling pools of brackish lava licking the walls of the newly formed precipice. That stuff is cool in cartoons, but not on my pizza.

—*Slice Harvester Quarterly*, Issue 7, "The Rest," visited on February 25, 2011

Opposite page: ABC No Rio, 156 Rivington Street

Making my way downtown (walking fast, faces pass, and I'm homebound doo doobee doot doot deeee dah dooble dooble dooble), I couldn't wait to get to the Lower East Side and eat at Mama's on Clinton Street, around the corner from ABC No Rio, the punkest place in New York City.

ABC is a once-squatted, now legit tenement building on Rivington Street next to the Streit's Matzo factory on the Lower East Side. It seems very importantly NEW YORK to me that the cool, long-running autonomous space is next to a matzo factory. I have so many memories of dozens of ratty punks sprawled across the sidewalk drinking Hurricane forties and eating matzo. Frankly, they should start putting matzo out in bars alongside the peanuts, because that shit goes well with beer, and it makes you hella thirsty.

In 1989, some folks started using No Rio to host Saturday afternoon hardcore matinees in an attempt to create a space for punk performance without the thuggish violence and homophobia of the CBGB Sunday Matinee crowd. They've put on shows at No Rio every week since then, and they still have a strict ideological policy for their bands: no -isms or -obias (racism, sexism, classism, ablism, homophobia, transphobia, etc.) in the lyrics, and no major-label acts. It's an amazing space and community resource, and in the nineties at least, it was an incredible place to be a teenager. I first learned about No Rio in 1996 as a thirteen-year-old lying on my bedroom floor, mesmerized by all the show fliers reproduced in the liner notes of Rancid's second album, *Let's Go!*

I daydreamed about the place for months before I got up the courage to actually go there. When I finally did, my teen BFF, Carly, walked me down from St. Marks to 156 Rivington Street, an address I had already memorized. Carly was a few months older than me, had a shaved head, and usually wore a homemade Heavens to Betsy T-shirt she had drawn with a Sharpie. I didn't have my first Mohawk yet, and I was still in that awkward phase between adolescent skate-poser and tween punk-poser. I had replaced my Airwalks with a pair of boots, but I was still wearing all my clothes two sizes too big, a symptom of having been raised by rap radio and having just seen the movie *Kids*.

Before we got to ABC, we walked into the bodega on the corner of Clinton and Rivington and bought forties, which I was amazed they would sell to us without even asking to see our IDs. I told myself I played it cool, but honestly, the bodega guys wouldn't have cared. No amount of playing it cool and pretending we looked grown-up could hide our baby faces.

I think the Skabs were playing that day, though I could be mistaken. No matter whether they played, they're the perfect band to stand in for my impressions of that whole punk scene back then. They were this terrifying vaudevillian street-punk band. The singer talked in a thick outer-borough accent but sang half the songs in Polish. Though it never materialized, the threat of violence hung ominously in the air for their entire set. They were fun and frightening, a fitting introduction to this subterranean world I desperately wanted to be a part of, although to be honest, I didn't really pay attention to the bands I saw at ABC back then, even though I went there almost every Saturday. Mostly I ate pizza, drank forties, and did drugs.

Remember that scene in *Pinocchio* where all the kids go to Pleasure Island and smoke cigars and play pool, and then eventually they grow donkey ears if they don't leave? That's what No Rio felt like (except that instead of donkey ears, you ended up with face tattoos if you stayed at ABC too long). It was awesome. For, like, five to seven hours every Saturday I was able to escape my mundane life in the suburbs and go to the city, where I was part of a ragtag gang of miscreants. Sure, I was too shy to really make any friends beyond the small crew of people I already knew, but it felt good just to be around a bunch of kids who also felt alienated by the world around us. And all that aside, it was a totally unsupervised place full of teens doing drugs and drinking, and there was loud, scary music and everyone looked like a cool freak. Who wouldn't want to be part of that?

There were a brief few years—let's say between ages nineteen and twenty-one—when I fell out of love with punk and decided it was childish and that I should grow up. During that time I stopped going to ABC entirely. Those were dark days. I believed in nothing. I grew a pompadour.

But around the time of that first Bent Haus show, I returned to the enveloping warmth of the Punx—my community, my gang, my family. Those among my new friends who had grown up around New York City had been at many of the same shows I had been to back in the day. We soon realized that none of us had talked to one another because we'd all been too shy or too drunk.

In the face of increased police and fire department pressure, stemming, I believe, from fear brought on by the fire at the Great White show in Providence, the No Rio Hardcore Collective abandoned its laissez-faire attitude toward teenage substance use in mid-2003, the same year St. Marks Pizza closed. Apparently that was the year that my first New York vanished. The hardcore matinees were now (mostly) booze and drug free. In return for free entry into the show, I would sometimes volunteer to stand watch in the backyard, politely asking anyone who was drinking to pour out their beers or to drink them elsewhere. The irony of a guy who had spent most of his teenage years dribbling puke down the front of his shirt in that very same backyard telling new teenagers not to drink wasn't lost on me, but the decision seemed prudent for the sustainability of the space, and that was my highest priority.

Whenever I went to No Rio as a teenager I would get a slice from New Roma, the horrible pizza parlor on the corner of Delancey and Essex. It was a total disaster of a place, and the food was disgusting, but the slice cost only a dollar, and there was a certain savage quality to the clientele that I found quite thrilling and appealing. When I returned to No Rio in my early twenties, some of my new friends heard I had been getting slices there and, appalled, brought me to Mama's pizza, a nice neighborhood joint around the corner on Clinton Street that served an absolutely ideal street slice—tangy, not-too-sweet sauce, crisp crust, good quality cheese, all working together in the delicate balance of ratios that separates a great slice from a mediocre one.

In 2006, on the anniversary of Joey Ramone's death, my old band Gloryhole played a set of Ramones covers at No Rio, and I invited my parents down to watch. I was twenty-three and had been playing in bands for almost ten years, but this was the first show I actually invited them to. After we played, when it got too weird to be hanging out with my mom and dad in the backyard of ABC, the site of so much of my teenage debauchery, we went around the corner to Mama's for a slice.

As we were talking, I mentioned my disdain for the current iteration of the Lower East Side, how inauthentic it seemed to me compared to the LES of my youth. Sure, it still presented itself as grimy, but it seemed disingenuous, like three-hundred-dollar jeans that are artfully stained with grease and dyes to look like the owner has been doing some kind of actual work in them.

"Man, this part of town has fuckin' changed in the past ten years, huh?" I said to my mom. "Remember when I was fifteen and you were scared for me to come here? Now Moby has a boutique tea shop around the corner!"

"Yeah, I do remember," she replied, "and it has changed, sure. But whose fault do you think that is?" She raised her eyebrows.

I looked at her, puzzled, "NYU? Giuliani?" I shrugged my shoulders in befuddlement.

"You, Colin. You and all your little friends coming down from the suburbs every Saturday to playact at being tough street kids. I know you guys thought you were so scary with your boots and Mohawks, but really you were just razing a clear path through a historically immigrant neighborhood for Moby to stroll down."

I didn't know what to say. I was shocked that my mother, of all people, had leveled such a scathing and insightful criticism at my revolutionary subculture, so I didn't say anything; I just stared down at my pizza.

She put her hand on my shoulder. "Look, that's just what

happens in cities. Neighborhoods change, they metamorphose; they're living things. I just want you to think about the part you play. Who can say if this change is for the worse or for the better?"

I certainly couldn't, although I knew it felt worse to me.

By February 2011, 380 slices into the project, it was time for me to head down that way to review pizza. I decided to call Kevers, a nice kid from Bay Ridge whom I've been friends with for many years. In my punk family tree, Kevers is the cousin I'm closest to. We might not see each other all that often, but when we do it's always a great time, and we remember why we're related. He's a little younger than me, and our teenage times at No Rio barely overlapped—although he does remember the days when drinking was still permitted and the backyard was a picturesque urban wasteland of teenage Mohawks and studded leathers.

Kevers is interesting and hard to pin down, though I can say he is the most effortlessly punk guy I know. It's not that he's got big, spiky hair or crazy clothes on (although when I met him ten years ago he was wearing a pair of bondage pants, a tuxedo shirt, a bow tie, and a bowler), but his outlook and general attitude toward life are perfectly punk. I'm not sure how to put this succinctly or to describe this indelible "punkness" to a layperson. If you don't get it already, you're probably never going to; but let me just say this: never in my life have I met someone more willing to walk around for hours looking for copper to scrap. Shit, maybe that just made it even more inscrutable.

Kevers has a Jewish father and an Irish-Catholic mother, just

like me, and the weird, jumbled-up name—Kevin O'Connell-Peller—
that comes with the territory. This cross-pollination, it seems, is
very typical of the outer boroughs. I'm not sure what facilitated
so much interethnic breeding in New York in the seventies and
eighties; maybe it's as simple as different immigrant communities
sharing the same neighborhoods. I do know that I like it. There's
something distinctly American, in a way I can be proud of, about
all these mutts running around together making new families.

When I met up with Kevers at the corner of Delancey and
Essex, it was pouring rain, a gloomy and overcast day at the tail
end of a piddling little winter. We were both incredibly hungover,
and thus hypercognizant of the stench of death and decay that
lingered over everything and everyone in the city. We sat in the
window of that horrid pizza shop from our youth, watching the
pedestrians on their continuous march toward death.

"I hate the future," Kevers said, taking a drink from his
scientifically enhanced water.

And I was all, "That is, like, the foundation upon which
everything we do is built! I wouldn't expect you to even say it
out loud. What makes you think you have to say something so
obvious?"

"I don't know." He looked around, sad but stalwart. "Maybe
it's the weather. Maybe it's sitting here looking out the window
at an advertisement for a Chipotle BBQ Bacon Angus McSnack
Wrap while I drink a Vitamin Water Formula Fifty and we talk
about how fun things used to be when we were teenagers. Maybe
it's something else."

And then our slice came up and we both realized the real
cause of our malaise. The future we hated so desperately in that

moment was not the distant threat of corporate monoculture, not the frightening new weather patterns and what they fore-told, but the more immediate future: the knowledge of how bad the pizza we were about to eat would actually be.

And so we ate that piece of pizza, even though we knew it would be terrible. It was. Yet we survived, like we always did, and continued on through the gloom. We ate at a few pizzerias we'd never been to, none of them particularly exceptional. We were just waiting until we got to Mama's, because that was our reward, our trusty ally waiting on Clinton Street.

We had eaten many slices at Mama's over the years, though our moments there had dwindled lately, as we both stopped spending so much time in Manhattan. The last time we had eaten there together was a year prior, on St. Patrick's Day, and nei-ther of us had been back since. That day, I had gone to Kevers's grandmother Winnie's apartment in Chelsea to have a raucous dinner with his whole clan. My grandmother had recently passed away, and I felt an urgent need to spend time with a rambunc-tious family in a tiny New York apartment. At Winnie's house, all my emotional demands were met. After eating and hanging out with the family for a while, we noticed that we had drunk almost half of Winnie's fifth of Philadelphia Blended Whiskey, and we decided to cut out and start walking home.

We left the building and began to walk east, leaning on each other for support, chummy like two characters in a Flann O'Brien novel. After walking a few blocks, I pulled a bottle of cheap port from my backpack.

"I bought this for your grandmother," I said as I brandished the bottle.

"Well, then why didn't you give it to my grandmother?"

"I forgot, I guess. Should I run back up?"

"If you want."

"I don't know, though. I mean, we already left; I wouldn't want to leave *twice*. That's not very dignified. And besides, other people may have left, too. What if I go back there and it's just Winnie, and she's watching TV or something and I disturb her, and she had been having a really perfect night and it was ending so well, and then all of a sudden I show up again and throw everything out of whack."

"I really don't think she'd mind, Colin . . ."

"Yeah, but what if she does? I think we should probably just drink it ourselves. Save her the trouble."

At this, Kevers grinned. "I think you're probably right."

We pulled the cork and each took a taste.

By the time we reached the base of the Williamsburg Bridge, we had finished the bottle, and despite our best efforts, no one had been willing to fight us. I knew I badly needed a pint of Old Grand-Dad from the liquor store on Delancey or I wouldn't be able to make it through the nearly two-mile walk across the bridge, but Kevers pulled me aside on Clinton Street, pointed at Mama's, and slurred, *"Wait. Weeneepissa."*

He was right. Neither of us had eaten in hours. We each got a slice and ate while standing in silence on the sidewalk. We devoured our meal, and when we finished eating I got my whiskey and we hit the bridge, and the rest of our night proceeded as you might expect, ending with both of us asleep on my stoop.

For the entire afternoon we spent together eating pizza for Slice Harvester, we rhapsodized about that slice we'd had a year prior. We saved Mama's for last because we knew it would be a nice contrast to our humble beginnings shoveling shit at New Roma. But when we approached, the facade was unrecognizable, and the sign read NONNA'S now. It was a similar-enough name, I guess—from mother to grandmother, from English to Italian. But nothing on the crisp, new awning held any of the schlubby charm of our old standby, and when we stepped inside, the décor was a faux-rustic Olive Garden disaster. It was clear that Mama's was gone for good.

I thought back to that slice a year earlier and asked the pizza man, "How long you guys been here?"

"I dunno." He looked up from the food he was preparing. "Two years, maybe."

"Are you sure?" I was startled. "I was here last year, and I could swear this was still Mama's."

"Well, I don't know what you been smokin', pal, but Mama's ain't been here in a while."

The slice at Nonna's was garbage. Maybe I was a little extra judgmental because I had been expecting a nostalgic favorite, but this piece of pizza was definitely, objectively no good. The cheese was the only acceptable thing about it, and that's all it was, acceptable. There was no sauce to speak of, and the crust was not only flavorless but crumbled to bits on the third or fourth bite.

And yeah, it's upsetting to see another one of my youthful favorite pizzerias turn into some soulless dump with a crappy slice, but that's just part of the ephemeral nature of New York. Sitting there with Kevers, I realized that even if the architecture and neighborhoods change, the people that you choose as your family are always gonna be there.

CHAPTER 12

Da Vinci Pizza

All told, this slice was totally satisfying, though not mind-blowing. But it was good, and I am happy to end on a positive note. I wouldn't go out of my way for this slice, but I stand behind it. I'll eat here the next time I spend an afternoon riding the ferry back and forth and reading. As we finished eating, Christina let out a huge belch, smiled, and said, "That was a burp of satisfaction."

—*Slice Harvester Quarterly*, Issue 7, "The Rest," visited November 22, 2011

Opposite page: The final slice

Getting through the LES was like zooming past the shortstop all the way to third base. With that neighborhood blacked out on my imaginary map, I could see home plate, and it was absolutely thrilling. I had one goal in mind: to get through the rest of this shit so I could eat the final slice with my hot, amazing, very patient girlfriend and then be done with it.

I had been seeing Tina for almost the entirety of the time I was Slice Harvesting, and I would sporadically ask her if she wanted to come along on a pizza mission. I felt like I wanted to introduce her as a character on my blog so that the throngs of *"ladies, fellas, and the people that just don't give a fuck"* (to quote a surprisingly gender-inclusive Limp Bizkit lyric) would stop throwing themselves at my feet, begging to date me. Just kidding—no one was begging to date me, but Tina was a really important part of my life, and Slice Harvester was so personal, and I just wanted her to be part of it.

But being from Miami, Tina has a flair for the dramatic. At first when I would ask, she would shoot me down with a grin. "Why would I wanna be part of your dumb project anyway?" It wasn't mean, it was flirty. I *liked* it. Maybe it's because I'm from New York, but when I'm thinking about my ideal partner, I want a lover *and* an adversary. Someone who's gonna challenge me when I'm fucking up, who will have strong opinions and express them, even fight for them; also, someone who can participate in the grand East Coast tradition of Busting Balls. To put it in perspective: I'm 99 percent sure "I Don't Wanna Walk Around With You" by the Ramones is a love song.

So I kept asking Tina if she wanted to join me, partially because I knew she liked it when I invited her, and partially because I liked it when she turned me down and gave me a little shit. Eventually she caved. I asked her to come along for some pizza, and she said, "Listen up, okay? You're gonna take me to eat the last slice. That's it. I don't wanna do some nothin', nobody slice in the middle of nowhere that don't mean shit in the grand scheme. I wanna eat the last one . . . if you're lucky enough to still be dating me." And she blew me a kiss as I headed out the door.

And listen: things with Tina were going more or less well. I was sticking to my moderation practice, at least when I knew I had to hang out with her. Some nights I wouldn't drink at all, and I didn't even notice it. But the fact remained that when I did let myself drink the way I really wanted to, I would REALLY DRINK, and there seemed to be no controlling it. I let this slide for a few months, and it seemed to have balanced out. I was only drunk some of the time, and I could keep it together when I wasn't.

On October 28, Tina picked me up from work, and we were walking around together holding hands and being cute. Slice Harvester was almost done, I hadn't been drunk in a few days, and she was congratulating me on how well I was doing. We decided that since I had become such a capable, functional adult, we should go have a couple of drinks to celebrate. Tina even said she didn't mind if I got drunk that night.

We got to the bar, and I just went for it. I had been given the green light, and there was no stopping me. Two hours later when Tina suggested that we head home, I threw a tantrum. She had given me permission to get drunk, and now she was trying to take it back. That was the sort of nonsense I wouldn't stand for. I ordered a round of shots for us, drank them both in defiance, and stormed out the door.

On the way back to my house I bought a six-pack. Tina went upstairs and went to bed immediately, without saying a word to me. I sat on my couch and drank four of the six beers in silent protest. How dare she try to control me! I passed out sitting up on the couch with the fifth beer open in my hand.

When I woke up in the morning with beer spilled all over me, surrounded by the cigarette butts I'd been angrily stubbing out on the floor, I went into my room to look for Tina to apologize, but she was already gone—though she'd left a note that said, "Call me when you get your shit together."

Standing in my apartment holding that note and thinking about what a baby I'd been the night before, I decided I wasn't going to drink anymore. No moderation. No week or month off to dry out with the intention of drinking again. I just wasn't going to drink at all. I was so sick and ashamed of myself for putting Tina through the irritating and volatile roller coaster of my alcoholism, which is what it was, and I could finally admit it. I rode my bike to Tina's house and let her know my decision. I expected her to be skeptical, but she was totally supportive. She accepted my apology and advised me to focus my attention on finishing up Slice Harvester so that I'd have something to think about besides the fact that I had just impulsively decided to quit drinking forever.

It wasn't easy, and it forced me to reexamine a lot of my relationships and a lot of the routines and patterns I'd built into my life, but quitting drinking was the best thing I could've done for myself. The months of moderation management, even if it wasn't a viable long-term solution for me, had prepared me for a life without booze. The most surprising thing about it was that I didn't really get any pushback from any of my friends. No one felt threatened by my sobriety; no one pressured me to drink. Everyone in my life uniformly supported my decision and did what they could to help me stick to it. The first couple of weeks were hard, and even with the couple of months of moderation, it took a little while before the fog in which I had been perpetually laboring lifted. But sometime in mid-November when I woke up clearheaded for the first time in as long as I could remember, I knew I had made the right choice.

Through this whole process, my pizza eating had slowed to a crawl. I posted only one pizza review for the entire month of October because I was too busy dealing with my own life. In the first week of November, I put up a post letting everyone know that I had four more pizza parlors left to review in all of Manhattan, two of which I had already eaten at. I was immediately approached by Aaron Rutkoff, a reporter from the *Wall Street Journal* who wanted to profile me for his horrible right-wing newspaper. I, of course, said yes, because I'm a narcissist and he was clearly a mensch, even if he was employed by White Demons. He wanted to come along with me to eat the last two slices of pizza, watch me work, and then write an article about it.

I asked Tina what she thought about the whole thing. I had been looking forward to just the two of us eating the last slice, and the idea of having a reporter along seemed to ruin the romance of it. She agreed, so I called the reporter and we decided that he would come along for the second-to-last slice but only send a photographer to the last. He wouldn't interact with us, just take pictures from afar.

On November 18, 2011, newsman Aaron Rutkoff accompanied me to Pranzo Pizza, at 34 Water Street, the very bottom of Manhattan, where we ate the second-to-last slice during the lunch rush, surrounded by Wall Street Goons stuffing their faces and storing up energy to Buy Low, Sell High or whatever those people do all day. I hadn't had a drink in three weeks, and I felt so lucid and articulate. I talked and talked and talked to this dude about New York, about pizza, about my life. I can't remember whether I talked to him about my recent sobriety, but if I did, it didn't make the article.

A week later, Tina and I took the subway down to Wall Street to eat the final slice. We held hands on the subway but didn't say much. She asked if I was nervous to be finishing, and I barely shook my head. The whole situation seemed unreal. Here I was, twenty-eight years old, almost a month sober, with this incredible woman who loved me despite myself sitting next to me on the subway holding my hand. We were going to meet a photographer from the *Wall Street Journal* to take pictures for a profile about me. I was just waiting for the other shoe to drop.

We got off the train and walked to the final place, Da Vinci Pizza, at 44 Water Street. My heart was beating so fast as we exited the subway, and I couldn't understand why. We followed the directions I'd hastily scrawled on the back of my hand (some things never change) until we took a right on Water Street and found ourselves standing in front of Pranzo Pizza.

"Is this it?" Tina asked, and I went into an intense panic. What if Pranzo was the last place? What if I had fucked something up and didn't count right or didn't do enough research, and I had already eaten at the last pizzeria with the stupid reporter and now I let Tina down *again* and, like, hell, maybe it wasn't that big a deal in isolation, but, like, this was a BIG DEAL because she and I had made it a big deal that she come eat the last slice with me and I had FUCKED IT UP AGAIN like I always do, what the fuck is wrong with—

"Or is it that place?" Tina interrupted my brutal inner monologue and pointed at a place half a block away, which we would've been standing in front of if we'd turned left on Water. I look down at the "L ON WATER ST" scrawled on the back of my hand and breathed a sigh of relief.

"It's that place," I told her, and we strode on over just as the photographer was arriving.

The inside of Da Vinci is tiled in faded pastels, with a greasy old letter board displaying the menu. It looks lived-in, the way I like a pizzeria to look—worn in like an old T-shirt. Tina and I ordered our slices and took a seat. We forgot all about the photographer taking our picture from a few tables away. I took a quick picture of my slice and pulled out my notebook.

"So, what do we do?" Tina asked.

"We eat the pizza," I said, lifting my slice to my mouth and gesturing that she do the same. "And we talk about it."

I felt a deep sense of relief when I took my first bite. This slice wasn't incredible, but it was certainly decent. It was a little thicker than I liked, with more dough and cheese than my ideal ratios, but not so much that it was overwhelming. Tina said, "It's got that youth-fair taste that I like." And she was right. This was like a better-quality New York version of a slice they would serve at a carnival—fluffy, delicious, and just what you need in the moment.

When we finished our slices, the photographer shook our hands and packed up. Tina put on her coat, but I just sat there. It was over. A little over two years ago, while I was drunk in the middle of the afternoon, listlessly coasting through my life, I had decided I was going to eat all the pizza in New York. Now here I was, sitting across the table from a woman I loved, who also loved me. I hadn't had a drink in almost a month; I felt better than I had in years. But I wasn't ready to let go.

Tina looked at me kindly. "You okay?"

"Yeah . . . I just . . . I don't . . ." I stammered.

"C'mon," she said. And she took my hand and led me to the subway home.

ACKNOWLEDGMENTS

FIRST AND FOREMOST:
Thanks to Christina Sparhawk for loving me when I was very difficult, teaching me how to love myself, teaching me how to be human.

TO EVERYONE WHO MADE THIS BOOK HAPPEN:
Jonathan Karp for offering me a book deal; Nina Pajak for telling her kid brother, Will Schwartz, to tell my kid sister, Emma Hagendorf, to tell me to respond to Jonathan's e-mail a week later; Dan Stein for giving me an office in his apartment and letting me keep the desk; Mya Spalter for helping me through this whole scary process; Julia Masnik for being my agent and fielding my constant neurotic questions; Sarah Knight for being an incredible editor/adversary/friend.

TO THE ILLUSTRATOR:
Thanks, Joe Porter, for singing in the most fun band I was ever in, and for illustrating all my zines and also this book.

TO MY BEST FRIENDS:
Milo Eadan, Caroline Paquita, Salvatore Gandolfo, Marcia Wiggley, and Nate Landry.

TO MY FRIENDS WHOM I WROTE ABOUT, AND EVERYONE ELSE WHO ATE PIZZA WITH ME:
Sweet Tooth, Cory Feierman, Nate Stark, Caroline (again), Phoebe and Greta Kline, Leah Kern, Kevers, Aaron Cometbus, Erick Lyle, Eliza Cutler, BBC, and all the resta yous.

TO MY WRITER/SELF-PUBLISHER CREW/GANG:
Ben Trogdon, Rancid Dave, Imogen Binnie, Golnar Nikpour, AC (again), Justin Sullivan, Corey Eastwood, Sarah McCarry, Lola Pellegrino, Cristy Road, Mimi Nguyen, Mike Taylor, Caroline (a third time).

THANKS TO THE FOLLOWING BANDS/RECORDS/SONGS/ RADIO PERSONALITIES:
Tear Jerks first tape, Jo Johnson *Weaving*, 50 Cent ft. The Game *Hate It Or Love It*, SZA *Z*, Nandas demo, Nicki Minaj *Pills N Potions* (admittedly, not her best work, but it just resonated so hard with me this year), Priests *Bodies and Control and Money and Power*, Arthur Russell *Love Is Overtaking Me*, Sinead O'Connor *I Do Not Want What I Haven't Got*, Funk Flex, Angie Martinez, Tom Scharpling.

Thank you to my mom, but not my dad. JK, bro. Luv u 4eva. Thanks to both my parents for raising me to be a weirdo.

I stole the name Slice Harvester from Greg Harvester's zine Rice Harvester; I stole the idea to steal the phrase "Times were rough and tough like leather" from Raekwon from Ben Pasternak's zine *Seventeen Forever*. That's probably all the stealing I did.

NO LOVE to cops, creeps, goons, buffoons, boneheads, birdbrains, shitfathers, dickwhippers.

MAD LOVE to all the punx, skins, rude boys and girls, greaseballs, dirtbags, and true weirdos all across the world. Stay fresh, stay strange. All you kids out there: keep the faith.

See you in the pit,

Lint

PS: I'm leaving someone out, I just know it, and I'm SOOOO STRESSED OUT about it, and if it was you, I'm sorry, okay? Just cut me some slack. Jeez.

ABOUT THE AUTHOR

COLIN ATROPHY HAGENDORF is an adult punk rocker and aspiring long-term soberdog. He loves eating pizza, working to dismantle systematic structures of oppression, and carefree afternoon naps. He collects obscure riot grrrl 7"ers and 1970s paperback editions of Sam Delany novels. He lives in Queens with three cats.